Copyright
Sep. 2018 Publishing

# HUMAN BEHAVIOR HOW INFLUENCES

## ROBOT DEVELOPMENT

JOHN LOK

Copyright © John Lok
All Rights Reserved.

# Contents

# Preface

Prepare

Nowadays, many businessmen or marketing research professional hope to apply different methods to predict consumer behaviors in order to know what will be future market activities and market changes to help them to choose to implement what kinds of marketing strategies more accurately. The methods include economic environmental change prediction method, consumer individual psychological change prediction method, micro or macro behavioral economic environmental change prediction method, marketing environmental change prediction method etc. different kinds of methods which can be applied to predict how consumer behavioral changes to influence whose behavioral consumption to the manufacturer products sale within one to two years short term or three to five years middle term, even above five years long term business plans. Hence, if the product manufacturers can apply the most suitable consumer behavioral prediction method to predict how consumers' choice will be changed to influence their products sale easily. It will have more beneficial intangible and tangible advantages to achieve the their product easier sale aim to ensure their businesses' future market share to be increased more easier to their countries' choice target sale markets. Otherwise, if they applied the inaccurate consumer behavioral prediction methods to predict how their consumers' behavioral changes wrongly. Then, it will influence their market shares to be same level, even it will decrease their market shares, when their consumer behavioral prediction inaccurately.

This book concerns to explain how and why human behavior may influence future robot continue develops. In my this book first part, I concentrate on indicate whether any artificial intelligence (AI) tools will be one kind of good consumer behavioral prediction method to be choose to apply to predict consumer behaviors. I shall indicate some examples, cases to give reasonable evidences to analyze whether (AI) tools will be one kind suitable tool to be applied to predict when and how consumer behavioral changes. If (AI) can be one kind tool to attempt to be applied to predict when and how consumer behavioral changes. Will it replace other kinds of methods to predict consumer behaviors? Does it have weaknesses to be applied to predict consumer behaviors, instead of strengths? Can it be applied to predict consumer behaviors depending on any situations of only some situation? Finally, I believe that any readers can find answers to answer above these questions in this book.

In my this book second part, I shall explain why and how human can possible apply (AI) tool to predict consumer individual emotion. I shall indicate case studies to explain how consumer individual better or worse emotion how to influence whose consumption behavior in different situation. Finally, I shall indicate evidences to conclude how and why (AI) tool that can be used to predict consumer individual emotion and it will have direct relationship to influence consumption behavior, as well as how (AI) tool can assist businessmen to judge whether what reasons case the customer does not choose to buy its product, it is possible because the product high price factor, poor product quality or poor staff service performance or attitude etc. different factors to influence the consumer decides to choose to buy the other product consequently, when the (AI) tool can confirm consumer has good or bad emotion to judge what factors are the causes his decision making at the moment.

Readers can understand why and how (AI) tool can be attempt to be applied to predict customer emotion and it can influence positive or negative consumption behavior to the product clearly in this part.

This book third part has these two research questions need to be answered? Can apply (AI) learning machine as well as micro and macro economic methods predict consumer behavioral changing?Can (AI) learning machine replace human marketing research method, e.g. survey or human psychological and micro and macro economic methods to predict consumer behaviors more accurate? The part indicates whether micro and macro economic methods can be attempted to apply to predict when, how and why consumer behavioral changing for every kind of different business. The second part indicates whether artificial intelligence can be attempted to apply to predict when, how and why consumer behavioral changing for every kind of different business.

In my this book fourth part, I shall considerate on businessmen and customers both beneficial view point to explain how to apply behavioral economic concept to predict how their specific industries marketing development trend or consumer behavioral changing trend in these micro economic (individual consumer psychological shopping change trend) and macro-economic (global every specific industry marketing changing trend) environment. This third part researches this two questions: Has it relationship between macro and micro economic environment change factors to influence marketing development change trend? Can businessmen apply macro and micro economic methods to predict future marketing development change trend in their specific industries?

In this book final part, I shall attempt to explain how and why human behavior may influence future robot needs whether any AI kinds of products may be influenced to increase or decrease.

# Prologue

Table of contents

● China share market investing behavior
Why has any individual country have many people invest share behavior which can influence the country's macro consumption desire?
Can technology influence human shopping behavioral change?

Why and how human behavior may influence the country's economic growth or recession? p.381-400

# ONE

# (AI) PREDICTION CONSUMER BEHAVIOR TOOL

1.1 How can artificial intelligent tools predict consumer behavior in vehicle market

What is (AI) consumer behavioral prediction tool? How any why will (AI) tool assist manufactures to attempt to predict consumer behavior before and after consumption occurrence? First, I shall indicate how to apply (AI) tool to predict vehicle product consumer behavior case example.

Nowadays, many vehicle manufacturers hope their vehicles can attract to vehicle buyers to choose to buy their vehicles. However, there are many different brands of vehicles to provide to them to choose, so the vehicle market competition is very serious.

How to judge their different kinds of vehicle price which is reasonable acceptance to attract vehicle buyers to choose to buy the brand of vehicle manufacturers' any kinds of vehicles, e.g. fast speed sport style vehicles, comfortable and slow speed common cars, for four passengers common small size or more than four passengers common large car size? How to evaluate the vehicle prices issue is important factor to influence vehicle buyers' choices. Either if the brand of vehicle price is too high to compare brands, it will influence many vehicle buyers choose to buy other brands' vehicles or if the brand of vehicle price is too low, it will influence vehicle buyers feel this brand's vehicle's quality is worse to compare to other vehicle brands' similar vehicle products.

Thus, if the brand of vehicle manufacturers can predict how to design vehicles which can attract many vehicle buyers to choose to buy whose any vehicle products. What are future vehicle buyers' favorable vehicle styles? Then, the vehicle manufacturer can concentrate on manufacturing the kind style of vehicle products to sell already. It will reduce its vehicle manufacturing investment risk.

How to apply (AI) tools to predict vehicle buyers' behavioral consumption model? Whether artificial intelligent tools can predict automotive buyers' behavioral consumption model and predict future trend. In fact, automotive brands and dealerships are facing an increasingly competition when attempting to manually gathering the vast quantities of data required to create customer focused programs that increase retention, ultimately new sales and service automotive business. Building a based on that client's intrinsic needs and interests to any kinds of automotive vehicles at any given time. This is especially true in the automotive industry where the time span between purchases is measured in years. Because vehicle buyers would not like often to change their old vehicle to another new one. So, their decisions to buying another new vehicle, the time is usually after one year, even longer time. Hence, it seems any vehicles won't be frequent consumption products to the owned at least one vehicle family consumers (vehicle buyers).

Hence, how to predict vehicle consumers' taste or preferable which styles of vehicle choices issues is very important. If the vehicle manufacturers can not manufacture any attractive vehicles to sell easily in this year. Then, it will lose time, money in this year because it won't know when the owned least one vehicle users or non-owned any vehicle users who will decide to buy one new vehicle or change another new vehicle ensure. The different brand vehicle dealers will possible wait more than one year to attract them to buy their vehicles if their styles are not attractive to compare other brands of vehicle competitors.

However, artificial intelligence and machine learning can help any vehicle manufacturers to find solution to solve patterns in highly to solve patterns in highly complex data-sets that are beyond the capability of a human brain, and then building and automatically acting on the customer insights it generates.

Given the automotive customer need for individualized communications, this technology is positioned to become a critical component of any successful vehicle retailer's domestic or/and overseas vehicle markets. How can vehicle manufacturers and retailers use (AI) to enhance their vehicle marketing campaigns? How will (AI) affect their vehicle sale marketing strategy? What criteria would they use when selecting on (AI) solution?

Vehicle consumers today are able to quickly access different brands of vehicle information, research vehicle products and reviews, negotiate prices and compare one vehicle brand or retailer to another resulting of the brands of vehicle customers. At the same time, the rise of " big -data mining", wearable devices that track user's every move and preference and greater contextualization in advertising and social media has resulted in consumer expectations of individualized. Thus, it seems that (AI) tools can be used to gather " big-data" and then they can make human's mind to analyze how to design kinds of vehicles to satisfy vehicle buyers' needs.

As automotive vehicle marketers can apply (AI) tools to achieve messaging strategies to meet the needs of this new generation of informed vehicle consumers, using data from a variety of sources to move from a variety of sources to move from mass- messaging to more personalized messages aimed at particular vehicle buyer segments, e.g. fast speed sport vehicle buyer segment, slow speed comfortable small size or large size of buyer segment. However, when 90% of vehicle marketers believe having a single vehicle buyer view is important, only 6% have achieved it.

However, one of the main issues vehicle marketers facing is the lack of capacity to efficiently sift through and analyze the massive vehicle buyer amounts of data required to create vehicle buyer individualized vehicle customer experiences easily. This is especially difficult for automotive dealers, the long periods between purchase cycles, and the highly considered nature of the vehicle purchase means that each vehicle dealer needs to not only track a large number of potential vehicle customers for an extremely long period of time, but each of those vehicle customers will generate a huge amount of different kinds of vehicle behavioral consumption data as they research their next vehicle purchase. However, by choosing the right (AI) technological tools and programs , vehicle dealers can solve this big data gathering challenge into a major advantage.

For Forrester vehicle brand example, vehicle consumers have more power over the Forrester vehicle brand's reputation than ever before. Mayne, L. (2014) indicated that Forrester calls this new (AI) tools is the " age of the vehicle customer", a 20 year business cycle in which the most successful vehicle enterprises will reinvent themselves to systematically understand and serve increasingly powerful vehicle consumers. To win in this new age,

Forrester declares companies must become vehicle customer obsessed and the only sustainable competitive advantage is knowledge and engagement with customers, such as (AI) gathering data knowledge.

Thus, the biggest challenge vehicle businesses currently face is not the collection of a large quantity of vehicle consumer data, but what to do with that data once they have it. Even at a large vehicle data research firm, the data sets are often too big for a single analyze, or even a team of analysts to sort through and draw conclusion from. However, enter artificial intelligence and machine learning , an efficient technology solution that can continuously find patterns in highly complex data sets that are way beyond the capacity of a human brain and then automatic drive action based on the customer insights is generated.

What is (AI) machine learning tool? Machine learning is a type of (AI) that learns from data and is not explicitly program. Think Amazon, face book. Machine learning serves up relevant content based on an individual vehicle purchase behavior and experiences. More simply, machine learning is a computer program that can learn relationships between data, subject those learnings to errors functions, and then learn from its errors. The program in effect, trains itself.

Lee, T. (2016) explained that "Thus, (AI) tools can learn deep a more advanced branch of machine learning inspired by how our brain's nervous function, has also been found to be especial effective in identifying patterns from data."

When this way sound is complicated from a vehicle dealer perspective, the implementation of a marketing program driven by artificial intelligence can take care of these tasks in an automatic vehicle fashion with little to no manual intervention required from the staff at time vehicle stores.

In practice at a vehicle dealership, the program will continue track vehicle customer behavior online, merging that data with any offline source ( like CRM or DMS data) and then analyze this aggregated vehicle buyer data set to predict what vehicle customer may be shopping for and what information they might like to relevance from different kinds style of vehicle design photos.

1.1 Why can (AI) be applied to predict consumer behaviors?

Artificial intelligence refers to complex in vehicle market, machine learning that posses the same characteristics of human intelligence and that have all our sense, all our reason and think just like human do. Besides, machine learning is the practice of using algorithms to collect and examine data, learn from it, and then make a determination or prediction about something in the world.

The machine is " trained" using large amounts of data and algorithms that give it the ability to learn how to automatically perform a task with increasing accuracy. Otherwise, deep learning is primarily based on artificial neural networks inspired by our understanding of the biology of human's brains.

Deep learning breaks down tasks in ways that enables machines to assist us with increasingly complex tasks, driverless cars, better preventive healthcare and more accurate product recommendation ( including vehicle recommendations). So, such as why (AI) technology can be applied to predict how vehicle consumer behavior changes to bring to judge whether vehicle consumer will like what kinds of vehicle styles next year. Then, vehicle manufacturers can gather overall vehicle consumer data to analyze and conclude the more accurate vehicle design direction for next year any new design vehicle manufacturing products.

Thus, (AI) machine learning can help vehicle manufacturers to solve how to design any new vehicle products challenge. A vehicle is both one of the most important and carefully considered purchases the majority of people will ever make in their lifetime. It is also a purchase that tends to be fundamentally tied to a person's identify and view of themselves. As the same time, vehicle consumers changing lifestyles result in changing vehicle needs, e.g. the young sport car enthusiast matures into the family driver.

Automotive dealers need to remember that vehicle customers and prospects are individual human beings with risk, complex and ever-changing lives factors, these factors will influence every vehicle consumer why who feels has vehicle purchase need, and how who choose to buy the first vehicle if who decided to buy the first vehicle.

The (AI) technological customer behavioral prediction tool seems to be the best vehicle salespeople in the world are those that know every one of their vehicle customers. Their likes and dislikes which style of vehicle design, preferences and changing tastes to vehicle choices. The capacity of the human brain, however, limits us from achieving this type of vehicle sales and frequent turnover at vehicle dealerships often results in the further loss of vehicle salespeople along with their vehicle customer relationships and knowledge. In this competitive vehicle environment, machine learning enables platforms to assist the vehicle sales team by tracking the vehicle consumer behaviors of each vehicle customer, learning and memorizing their preferences and predicting their future vehicle purchase needs.

Finally, I recommend that for a vehicle dealerships marketing platform to make their customer engagement efficient and fully-functional, I should be able to: applying (AI) tools to track every vehicle customer behavior across the web, connecting to a society of data sources, CRM, DMS, third-party, web vehicle brands, social email, click etc., aggregating and accurately cross-reference data from a variety of sources, leveraging this data to drive insights on a mass scale, as well as on an individualized basis, driving actions and automatically direct customer engagement via multiple channels based on where each customer is in their individual lifecycle.

1.2 How can (AI) provide businesses with better-informed decisions

I shall explain how (AI) technology can provide businesses with better-informed decisions to drive top-line growth, deliver meaningful experience for customers and smooth their path along the consumer journey. The widely understood definition of (AI) involves the ability of machines or computers to learn human thinking, reasoning and decision-making abilities.

A Narrative science study in 2015 year identified that (AI) was being used primarily in voice recognition, machine learning virtual assistants and decision support. This study also highlighted the many branches of (AI) and that techniques and their definition are used interchangeably. It is possible that (AI) can be used to gather big data , then to analyze to help businesses to predict consumer behaviors. For example, one of the most common techniques is machine learning, where algorithms are used to perform tasks by learning from historical data. Another growth branch of (AI) is natural language procession.

However, during 2017 year, search engines will begin to factor additional behavioral data into prediction of customer behavioral results, such as the user's history of searches and locations and previously captures conservations. Artificial intelligence will use this information to power predictive search results, e.g. predictive future consumer's choice behavioral processing for any kinds of businesses.

Predictive search will improve the quality of search results, and provide new insights into consumers' behavior and the moments which matter to them. Search will give recommendation into tailored how consumer individual choice in consumption process. Several of the largest online platforms already use machine learning to improve predictive consumer behavioral search results.

For example, Google's rank brain technology adds research by understanding the context in which the consumer has entered it. Over time, rank brain will learn further from user behaviors Amazon's DSSTNE ( pronouned destiny) learns from shoppers' purchasing habits and consumption behavior to offer better product recommend actions, which Amazon can offer before a consumer has entered anything into the search bar. However, this technology is not independent of human input. For example, Google engineers will periodically retain the rank brain system to improve the models it uses. For another example, in 2016 year , Apple computer revamped its photos app to allow consumers to search for specific items in the phots, they want to find, not just dates and locations. Each photo that an intelligent phone or intelligent pad user takes goes through 11 billion computations, so that photos can understand exactly what is the photography.

It seems that in future, (AI) machine learning will allow search to evolve even further. Search engineers will deliver refined recommendations to their business users and use less human input to predict consumers' needs. For IBM computer example, it indicated 90% of the data that exists today has been created in the last two years. This huge explosion of data gives brands the opportunity to quickly spot and react to the latest trends, fashion and fads among its clients and potential clients. This will allow companies to better engage with younger consumers, who gain influence access to the latest trends, and use the brands. They associate with to help define who they are as individuals. Thus, brands have to identify and make use of them before consumers move on, but the vast quantity of data available makes. This a resource-intensive task. For next example, Lesara, a based online clothes store, uses this machine learning to inform its product decision often gathering information from internal and external sources. When its trends -spotting shoes. Lesara has a range of over 20 styles and sells hundreds of pairs a day. It focus on giving consumers, the very latest trends allow Lesara to develop on average of 50,000 new items each year. It compared to 11,000 old items each year. Thus, (AI) brain seems to human brain to own analytical ability to predict consumer behaviors.

For another example, Lesara is one online clothes store, uses machine learning decisions after gathering information from internal and external sources. One of its most popular products, shoes with LED started life when its trend spotting software flagged up a blogger wearing similar shoes. Now

Lesara has a range of over 20 styles and sells hundreds of pairs a day. Its focus on giving consumers the very latest trends allows Lesara to develop an average of 50,000 new items each year, compared to 11,000 for its competitor Lara. it seems (AI) machine learning can help Lesara business to predict what kinds of shoes design or style that shoe consumers will prefer choose to buy in future shoe market trend. Thus, Lesara can predict shoe consumers' taste successfully and it can manufacture many attractive style of shoes. (AI) machine learning can gather global past shoe consumer's shoe shopping experiences, then analyzes to make conclusion to give lesara recommendation successfully. This will make the experience more enjoyable for shoe consumers and allow Lesara to advert whose different new style or design of shoes to deliver them move relevant messages by understanding the context of the experience.

However, (AI) machine learning will have this risk who manufacturers need to concern if they applied this technology to predict consumer behavior. It is on sample consumers' privacy issue, in order to avoid complaint chance occurrence. However, machine learning can tie this data together to identify which f the billions of devices are being used by individual consumers. This helps brands understand how consumer engagement and actions can be attributed to different messages in different contexts and at different time. So, machine learning can help brands to build confidence to promote their products by any advertisement channels. When, this new (AI) machine learning technology can conclude how to design their products to be the most attractive, due to it has more accurate to predict consumer behaviors to compare human themselves prediction judgement effort. It seems that (AI) machine judgement effort is more accurate to compare to human judgment effort.

For example, google is moving away from cookies and using logged in data to track and make to users. It plans to expand the scope of the brand lift tool from online video. Thus, consumers are responded will to shippable context, finding it persuasive and easy to navigate by (AI) machine learning decision. For example, fashion brands can aggregate their You tub videos and blogs into a mobile context marketing experience, such as brand centric context into a personal shopping activity gives the shopper an experience, who are likely to remember and tell their friends about any new style of products design promotion from these internet advertisement channels after (AI) machine learning tools' styles of product design recommendation.

# **TWO**

# WHAT IS (AI) DEEP LEARNING TECHNIQUES TO FORECAST ENVIRONMENT BEHAVIORAL CONSUMPTION

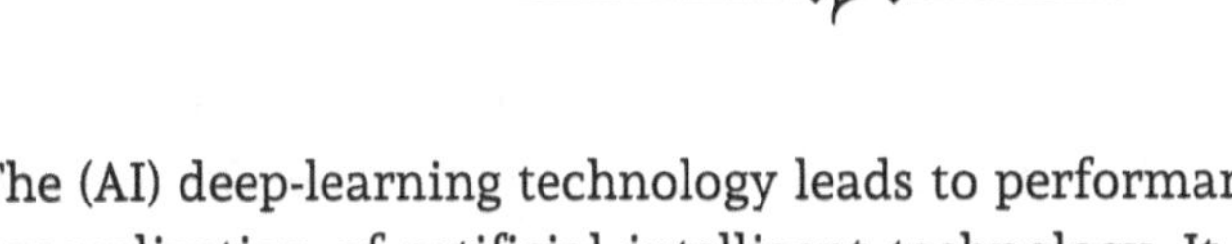

The (AI) deep-learning technology leads to performance enhancement and generalization of artificial intelligent technology. It influences the global leader in the field of information technology has declared its intention to utilize the deep-learning technology to solve environmental problems, such as climate change. So, it will help agriculture farming businesses can raise any plant food: vegetable, fruit, rice which grow up very easily if farmers can apply (AI) deep-learning technology to solve environment problems to influence their plant food grow. If the whole year seasonal change is very good and it is suitable for any plant food to grow in farming land easily, e.g. rain is enough and soil is enough for any plant food to grow in the farm lands. Then, fruit, rice, vegetable etc. agriculture businesses will have much beneficial attribution to global farmers.

The question is how to use deep-learning technologies in the environmental field to predict the status of pro-environmental consumption. We predicted the pro-environmental consumption index based on Google search query data, using a recurrent neural network ( RNN model). To certify the accuracy of the index, we compared the prediction accuracy of the RNN model with that of the ordinary least square and artificial necessary network models. For example, the RNN model predicts the pro-environmental consumption index better than any other model. we expect the RNN model to perform still better in a big data environment because the deep-learning technologies would be increasingly as the volume of data grows. So, deep-learning technologies could be useful in environmental forecasting to prevent damage caused by climate change to influence any rice, vegetable, tomato, potato, fruit etc. different plant food grow in any countries' farming land easily.

For South Korea example, over 800 government agencies spent 2.2 trillion Korea won on eco-products in 2014 year. However, green products are rarely purchased outside these agencies. This phenomenon occurs because there is a gap between consumer attitudes and behavior , that is environmental attitude is a major factor in decision making vis-a-vis the consumption of " green" food and services ( Jorea Ministry of Environment, 2015). Therefore, it is necessary to understand those consumer attitude, that will lead to sustainability-conductive behavior and consumption.


2.1 Environmental consumption prediction

Recently, many researchers have studied pro-environmental consumption and household indexes as well as suicide rate predictions using messages posted by internet users on Google trend, Tweets etc. channel. Whether can environmental consumption be predicted by (AI) deep-learning technological internet channel? How can impact the pro-environmental consumption attitudes of green policies? Korea scientists estimated pro-environmental attitudes using search query data provided by Google trend and confirmed through regression analysis, that pro-environmental attitude has a positive correlation with the pro-environmental attitude index. They also explained that environment-friendly attitude of residents plan an important role in policy making. In the past, most household consumption indexed were calculated through surveys, but (AI) deep-learning technological tool " big data" have recently gained research attention ( Lee et al. 2016).

It seems that (AI) deep-learning technology can help agricultural export countries' farmers , e.g. US, UK, Canada, New Zealand, Australia, Japan, China, India etc. they can predict environmental behavioral consumption to any rice, tomato, potato , fruit, vegetable etc. plant food consumers. The beneficial advantages to them include as below:

(a) Assuming they know their countries' weather, when it has less rain to cause drought or when it has more rain in any seasonal time in the year. They can choose not to grow any kinds of above these plant food to avoid loss.

(b) They can make any kinds of above these plant food price raising after their prediction of these bad seasonal time to cause their plant food shortage supply challenge. Because these plant food consumers' demand number is more, but the supply of these above plant food supply number is less. However, due to they had predicted when the bad seasonal time can not allow them to grow these above plant food before. So, they have enough time to grow many these above plant food number in predictive good seasonal time to prepare to supply to their plant food import countries' plant food consumers to eat. Thus, these predictive environmental consumption plant food export countries can raise their plant food price to sell to them. When, the other non-pre-predictive environmental consumption plant food export countries can not supply any one of those plant food to them to eat, due to the bad climate to cause them can't grow any one of these plant food to export to sell.
Thus, (AI) deep-learning technology can be applied to predict how to raise the plant food supply number in order to raise price to the import plant food countries consumers to eat, due to they feel difficult to buy these plant food to eat in the bad climate seasonal time in whole year.

(c) (AI) deep-learning technology can help climate scientists to find what reasons cause their countries; rain sudden increases or cause their countries' rain sudden decreases. After its gathering data analysis, it can assist climate scientists to find solution methods to attempt to control the rain level can be right falling down level to let agricultural export farmers who can grow their plant food to sell to agricultural import countries in whole year.

(d) The agricultural export countries' farmers can apply (AI) deep-learning technology to help them to choose whether growing which kinds of plant food in that whether climate time to earn more plant food consumption number more easily.

Due to the agricultural countries climate will often change, for example, tomato, potato, rice, fruit etc. plant food can be adapt to grow in more rain time, but vegetable can not be adapt to grow in more rain time. If farmers can apply this technology to predict when it will have move rain or when it will have less rain to fall down in their countries. Then, they can choose to grow which kinds of plant food number more, in the suitable seasonal climate time in order to raise plant food growing number productivities to supply to sell to satisfy any agricultural food import countries' demand effectively.

(e) (AI) deep-learning technology can help agricultural import countries to solve agricultural food shortage challenge in long term. When this technology can be popular to base applied by the agricultural plant food export countries. It will solve global agricultural food shortage challenge. For example, when one agricultural export countries' farmers can popular accept to apply this technology to predict when to grow which kinds of plant food more to rise number productivities to sell. e.g. vegetable, fruit, rice Besides another agricultural export countries' farmers can also accept to apply this technology to predict when to grow plant food, e.g. potato, tomato to raise number productivities to sell. Then, they can concentrate on growing the specific kinds of plant food in order to raise the specific plant food number productivities in every seasonal change time every month. Then, global agricultural plant food supply must be raised, due to these predictive environmental change farmers can know who ought grow which kinds of plant food to sell to raise number productivities.

2.2 How can apply (AI) digital channel to predict consumer behaviors?

(AI) digital channel can be applied to help businesses to evaluate whether how much the product price is the most attractive to persuade consumers feel it is the most reasonable price to sell. It helps consumers to feel which brands of products which ought change the price to let consumers to choose to buy the brand of product. It can be applied to predict whether how many consumer numbers can be increased or decreased when the brand of product's price is variable. It aims to give opinions to help any brand of product manufacturers or sellers to judge whether which price is the most reasonable to let consumers to accept to choose to buy the brand of product in popular.

Thus, (AI) price measurement technology can be preference to be applied online communication ecommerce and mobile phone internet platform aspect. As businesses can enter their past products prices data and past customer number data into computer or mobile. Then, (AI) price measurement technology can gather these data to analyze these product prices and past customer number to compare their prices variable changing range level to find their price variable difference to measure to make conclusion about every product's price variable changing will influence how many customer number increase or decrease changing to choose to sell their different kinds of products more accurate. Then, (AI) price measurement software will help them to analyze all past price variable changing data to compare whether which price range can let customers to feel it is more reasonable and attractive to influence them to choose to buy the product among different brands of product choice.

Because any product's price is one important factor to influence consumers to choose to buy the product, instead of quality, durability, shape, appearance, color, brand familiarity etc. factors. Any online businesses with a focus on Asia should considerate (AI) customer care, and virtual shopping experience, whereas is Europe and North America still value face-to-face and/or real human interaction over (AI) or virtual worlds.

For example, Amazon publish has applied (AI) price measurement technology to help authors to decide how much every different topic of e-book or paper book price, it can attract the largest number of readers to buy. Any one author only needs to type whose book name to Amazon publish author himself/herself Amazon website. Amazon publish (AI) price measurement learning machine will help them to auto-calculate and judge how much e-book or paper book price is the most attractive and the most reasonable in order to increase reader number to buy their e-books or paper books to read. So, (AI) online price measurement machine will gather past similar book names and past every similar book readers' reading times and the number of readers to give opinions to let every author to judge whether his/her very new e-book or paper book ought charge how much price to the e-book or paper book which can attract many readers to choose to buy. Although, it is not ensure that the e-book or paper book price must let readers to feel it is the most reasonable price to choose to buy in reader's view point. However, it has other factors to influence readers' choice to buy the e-book or paper book, e.g. whether the book content is attractive to public, the author's familiarity, the book's page is enough or not to satisfy readers to read etc. factors. But, instead of all these extra factors to influence readers to choose to buy the book to read. (AI) price measurement learning machine can real give opinions to every author to let them to judge the e-book or paper book different price range whether is too high to influence readers to choose to buy to read or tool low to influence readers feel it is possible poor content book to compare other similar content books. Thus, (AI) price measurement machine can help authors to predict every reader's reading behaviors or reading experience and reading habit from online channel in short time easily. The author only enter the book name to let Amazon publish price measurement machine to check, it will follow past reader's reading habit and reading experience to judge whether the similar all book topic sale record to judge how much price is the reasonable price to attract many readers to buy the book.

Hence, (AI) can be applied to digital channel to help businesses to predict consumer behavior in the future. In the future, mobile/smartphone, laptop, desktop will be most frequent used ecommerce channels to develop online business. So, (AI) can be also applied to these platforms to gather data to make analysis to help businesses to predict consumer purchase behaviors popularly. Due to , ecommerce is popular to global, so digital online and instore channels can be one good channel to let (AI) learning machine to make platform to gather past every online consumer purchase ( buying) experience data to help businesses to build brand personality and having a responsible, positive impact on society.

To apply (AI) learning machine technology to understand customer online purchase behavior, it will raise business e-commerce successful chance: For example, (AI) learning machine can help businesses to gather data to analyze to determine whether short-term or long-term signals in the online consumer behavior that indicate higher purchase intents to let every online business to know. (AI) learning machine can find that online users with long-term purchasing intent tend to save and click through on more content.

However, as online users approach the time of purchase their activity becomes more topically focused and actions shift from saves to searches from online consumption channel. Then, (AI) learning machine will further find that the brand product purchase signals in online behavior can exist weakness before an online purchase is made and can also be traced across different online purchase categories. Finally, (AI) learning machine synthesize these insights in predictive models of online user purchasing intent to the brand of product. Taken together, it's work identifies a set of general principles and signals that can be used to model online user purchasing intent across many online content discovery applications. Thus, (AI) learning machine can help online businesses to gather any online users' click online behaviors data to judge whether there are how many online users will choose to find their online business websites to make final decisions to buy their products from online channels. Then, it will give opinions to help the online businesses to let it to judge whether what are the important website factors will help its online business to attract many online consumers, e.g. designing unattractive website issue, online unattractive product photos issue, unclear website color issue, unclear website advertisement message, contents and words impressions issue, lacking image movement frequent attractive seeing issue etc. different website factors. Thus, online digital channel will be one good choice to apply (AI) learning machine to help businesses to predict consumer behaviors.

2.3 Can apply artificial intelligent learning machine " big data" gathering method to predict manufacturers' behavioral performance ?

In consumer view point, can they apply (AI) learning machine to predict manufacturers' behavioral performance to judge whether whose products are value to buy. Nowadays, (AI) and big data are reshaping the risk in consumer privacy. For example, consumers want to hide their willingness to pay just as firms want to hide their real marginal cost, and buyers have less favorable information, say a low credit shore, prefer to withhold it just as sellers want to conceal poor product quality. So, it implies that it is possible (AI) learning machine can help customers to gather any manufacturers' past sale performance, e.g. how many complaints or appreciation from clients, product quality etc. sale data to let consumers to make judgement whether it is value to buy to compare other competitors. So, it has risk to the poor product quality of manufacturers. Otherwise, it has benefits to the good product quality of manufacturers. It also implies all manufacturers' privacy is not protected or secret when (AI) learning machine is popular to be used to predict manufacturers' behaviors by consumers.

Information economists suggest that both buyers and sells have an incentive to hide or reveal private information, and these incentives are crucial for market efficiency. Data technology that reveals consumers type could facilitate a better match between product and consumer type, and data technology that helps buyers to assess product quality could encourage high quality production.

Thus, (AI) big data technology can also assist consumers to gather different manufacturers' data to compare what their advantages and disadvantages of their products are. Then, consumers can make comparison to choose which brand of product is the suitable to whom to buy in these more choice consumption market. (AI) learning machine will gather similar brand their products' data to analyze to make conclusion to let consumers know or feel to make final judge to find what advantages or disadvantages of these sample brands of similar products' comparison from internet. On the other hand, it means that manufacturers can gather consumers' past purchase behaviors or purchase experience from (AI) big data gathering method to record and analyze to give opinions to let manufacturers to know what reasons or factors influence consumers choose not to buy their products from internet.

(AI) big data gathering consumer behavior prediction method can give these benefits to manufacturers and consumers both, such as: New concerns arise because (AI) technological advance which have enables reducing cost of collecting, storing, processing and using data in mass quantities extend information beyond a single transaction. These advances are often summarized by the big data, it means charge volume of transaction-level data that could identify individual consumers by itself or in combination with the datasets.

The popular (AI) takes big data as in input in order to understand, predict and influence consumer behavior. Modern (AI) is used by legitimate companies, could improve management efficiency motivate innovations and better match demand and supply. But (AI) in the wrong hand, also allows the mass production of fraud and deception. Since , data can be stored, traded and used long after the transaction. Future data use is likely to grow with data processing technology, such as (AI) big data gathering consumer and manufacturer behavioral prediction method from internet channel.

Thus, future (AI) big data learning machine can also help consumers to choose the best brand of manufacturer's products among different brands of manufacturers products choice to compare their past sale performance from internet. They can apply (AI) big data statistic method to gather all different manufacturers' similar products past sale data to compare their advantages and disadvantages to make the best decision to choose to buy which brand of product is the most suitable to them to buy to use. It seems (AI) big data can also help consumers to predict any manufacturers' manufacturing behaviors or manufacturing performance whether they are improving their product quality or are deteriorating their product quality.

Thus, (AI) big data tool is also important to help customers to predict future the different brands of manufacturer performance will have improvement in possible.

Thus, I believe that artificial intelligent "big data" gathering method can be suggested to be applied to attempt to predict consumer behavioral changes in global business environment, the reasons are as below:

On the consumer's beneficial hand, Consumers can apply this method to attempt to gather any global manufacturers data to be analyzed by this artificial intelligent learning system. Then, it analyzed all the different brands of specific similar product manufacturer' data to compare what are the range of the best past manufacturing history and sale data to the group of best manufacturers, and what are the range of the better past manufacturing history and sale data, and what are the range of the good past manufacturing history and sale data, and what are the range of the common past manufacturing history and sale data. Finally, the (AI) learning system will compare all the specific similar product, e.g. mobile phone or computer, television, car etc. different kinds of specific products of global manufacturers to conclude the result is such as whether which brands will be the best manufacturers to let the consumer to buy the television or mobile phone or computer or car etc. different kinds of products. It can make more accurate judgement to compare general human's phone or questionnaire surveys investigation method, newspapers, television, radios, internet searches etc. different manufacturing news or data gathering channels to find which brands are the most worth confidence to consumers to choose to buy the specific product in the global consumption market.

On the manufacturers' beneficial hand, manufacturers can apply (AI) data gathering method to predict consumer emotion and buying behavioral changes more accurate. For example, the vehicle manufacturer, it plans to gather data to predict potential driving fast speed sport vehicle consumers' preferences trends in order to make the accurate judgement how to design its sport vehicles to attract many sport vehicle buyers who will choose to buy it's brand of any driving fast speed sport vehicles. It can attempt to apply (AI) intelligent learning system to gather global different brands of sport vehicle data concerns that all past driving fast speed sport vehicle buyer's preference of sport vehicle design. Then, the (AI) intelligent learning system gather global different brands of driving fast speed sport vehicle which had ever been purchased by the different country's driving fast speed sport vehicles consumers. After, it can compare divide the range of similar driving fast speed sport vehicle design and similar price to be different groups. The (AI) intelligent learning system can attempt to follow the past number of different brands of driving fast speed sport vehicle buyers to calculate how many driving fast speed sport vehicle buyers who choose to buy the brand of driving fast speed sport vehicle as well as it will analyze and make judgement to find whether the cheaper price reason attracts the different countries sport vehicle buyers choose to buy the brand of driving fast speed sport vehicle or the attractive design reason attracts the different countries sport vehicle buyers choose to buy the brand of sport vehicle or fast speed reason attracts the sport vehicle buyers choose to buy the brand of sport vehicle.

For example, although some brands of driving fast speed sport vehicle manufacturers' prices are very high, but they can still attract global many sport vehicle consumers to buy. Whether all sport vehicle's attractive design is the main factor to influence them to buy or whether it's fast speed is the main factor to influence them to buy or whether it's safe confidence it the main factor to influence them to buy or it's familiarity brand is the main factor to influence them to buy. (AI) intelligent learning system will attempt to make judgement and analysis to conclude whether the attractive design factor is the main factor to influence many sport vehicle consumers to choose to buy the brand of sport vehicles.

Otherwise, for another example, although some brands of driving fast speed sport vehicle manufacturer's prices are low, but they can not still attract many global many sport vehicle consumers to buy. Whether all vehicle's unattractive design is the main factor to influence them choose not to buy their fast speed driving sport vehicles or whether the unsafe factor is the main factor to influence them choose not to buy their fast speed driving sport vehicles or whether unfamiliarity brand is the main factor to influence many consumers choose not to buy their fast speeding sport vehicles.

Thus, when (AI) learning system had helped the fast speed sport vehicles manufacturer to gather all different brands of fast speed driving sport vehicle's past sale data and price data, design of different sport vehicle, e.g. color choice, method of style, comfortable chair styles and chair sizes and what kinds of steel material to manufacture the sport vehicles data and driving safe and accident occurrence data and the data concerns what reasons of the past complaint to brand of sport vehicle manufacturer from its sport vehicle buyers. Then, it can make more conclusion to give more accurate opinions whether which brands of fast speed driving sport vehicle manufacturer(s) whose sport vehicle design is the main factor to attract consumers choose to buy its any driving fast speed sport vehicle products really. Thus, it seems that it can make more accurate judgement to compare television survey, questionnaire survey to gather data concerns how to design the fast speed sport vehicle to attract consumers to choose to buy the sport vehicle manufacturer's planning sport vehicle products. I believe that (AI) learning system can help the sport vehicle manufacturer to make more accurate conclusion or judgement how to design its fast speed driving sport vehicles to attract it's consumers more easily.

# THREE

# (AI) TOOL PREDICTS CONSUMER IMMEDIATE AND EXPECTED EMOTION HOW TO INFLUENCE CONSUMPTION DECISION

If (AI) tool can be confirmed to apply to predict consumer behavior, then I can conclude that it can be attempted to apply to predict what the factor(s) of the product itself can cause the consumer has positive or negative emotion, so the manufacturer can attempt to avoid the bad factors cause to bring negative emotion to influence the consumer chooses not to buy the product more easily, such as vehicle product case.

Economists refer to the consumption desirability is as " utility" and the product or service consumption decision making is arose

influenced by maximizing utility only. However, they neglect consumer individual immediate emotion change will also influence the consumer individual consumption decision consequently. Expected emotions are those that are anticipated to occur as a result of the outcomes associated with different possible courses of action. For example, if a potential investor, were deciding whether to purchase a stock, who might imagine the disappointment who would feel if who ought it and it reduced its price. Otherwise, whose emotion would experience , such as regret if it increased in price, but who does not buy it before the stock rise its price. However, I believe nowadays technology, in the future one day, (AI) tool can be attempted to assist consumer psychology profession or marketing research profession to assist them to find what are the bad factors to influence consumers choose not to buy any manufacturers' products. Then, when the manufacturer

can discover what are the bad factor(S) cause(S) consumers who do not choose to buy their products, then the manufacturer can raise whose product of consumption desirability or " utility" to raise whose product's consumption decision making is influenced by maximizing utility. Hence, (AI) tool will be possible to find what the bad factor(S) to cause consumers do not choose to buy the manufacturer's product in order to raise the product's utility to bring consumer positive emotion to choose to buy its product in possible. SO, (AI) tool will be one consumer psychological emotion prediction tool to assist any manufacturers

to help their products to build positive emotion to any consumers in possible.

The key feature of expected emotions is that they are experienced when the outcomes of a decision materialize, but not at the moment of choice, at the moment of choice, they are only feel about future emotion. Such as consumption case, if the consumer chose to buy the product or consume the service before it's price is increased. Then, the consumer will feel happy and it is worth to purchase or consumer the service as well as the consumer's expected emotion is positive before who decides to buy the product or consume the service, because who believes or feels the product or service's price will be raised in short term, e.g. after one month, one week. Thus, it means that if the consumer does not believe or

feel or predict the product or service's price either it will increase or decrease in short term, whose emotion will be negative, those negative emotion will influence who does not decide to buy the product or service, it is possible that who feel it is not worth to buy the product or consume the service immediately. He She will choose to consume the service or buy the product to wait it's price is decreased later. it seems that the consumer's positive or negative emotion will influence who decides to buy the product or consume the service later or earlier. Thus, it has close relationship between the consumer individual immediate purchase or consumption decision and positive emotion or negative emotion ( either expected emotion or immediate emotion influences).

Consequently, if (AI) tool can help any manufacturers

to predict when its product price ought to be increased or decreased in order to attract consumer to choose to buy its product. Then, it can help any manufacturers to build positive expected emotion to attract consumers to choose to buy its product more easily. For example, when the (AI) tool can predict when the consumer expects the product price will fall down, then it can give ideas to the manufacturer to raise up the product price in the month, then it predicts many consumers expect the product price will fall down after six months. So, the product price will not be fall down after six months. So, many consumers will feel disappointment and they will choose to buy the product if the manufacturer

decided to raise the product price after six months. Then, the higher product price will cause many consumers worry about the product price will continue rise up, so they will prefer to choose to buy the product immediately after six months because they afraid the product price will continue to rise up in the year. Then, I assume that (AI) tool has effort to predict when consumers feel the product will rise up or fall down, then it can give ideas to the manufacturer when to rise up or fall down the product price in order to attract or persuade many consumers choose to buy the product in different period in the year.

1.1 What does (AI) tool predict immediate emotion mean?

Psychologists indicate that immediate emotions, by contrast, are experienced at the moment of choice and fall into one of two categories. Integral emotion, like expected emotions, arise from thinking about the consequences of one's decision, but " integral emotion", unlike expected emotions are experienced at the moment of choice. Such as purchase stock case, the share buyer might experience immediate fear at the thought of the stock's losing value. " Incidental emotions" are also experienced at the moment of choice, such as a consumer predicts the product or service price whether it will be risen up or fallen down. If he/she feels the product or service price will fall down after next month and he/she will choose to buy the product or consume the service. But consequently, after next month, the product or service's price won't fall down absolutely.

Then, he/she will have incidental emotion to influence whom to choose whether he/she ought buy the product or consume the service, due to the product or service price is not still fall down. Otherwise, he/she is fear the product or service will not fall down in short term. Even, it will increase price later. Hence, whose incidental emotion will have possible to influence whom to choose to buy the product or consume the service after one month, if the product or service's price is still not increased absolutely. So, (AI) tool can be attempted to apply to predict when the product price ought need to be raised or fallen down in order to attract consumers to choose to buy the manufacturers' product in different period.

Economists indicate utility an individual consumption with an outcome might arise from a prediction of emotion: For example, a dinner eater might choose a higher utility to an Italian restaurant dinner than a French restaurant dinner because who anticipates being happier at the former, even the former's dinner price is higher than the French restaurant.

So, such as this restaurant dinner case, if one (AI) tool can assist the French restaurant owner to find what factor(S) cause(S) the dinner consumers do not choose to go to its restaurant to eat its food, e.g. high price factor, bad taste factor, bad wait service performance factor, bad cooker's cooking skill factor, poor advertisement promotion factor, poor familiar factor, poor location or poor eating environment etc. different factors. Then, the French restaurant owner can find methods to avoid the bad factor(S) cause(S) many dinner consumers do not choose to go to whose French restaurant to eat dinner more easily.

The question is that whether the positive emotion factor can influence the consumer changes whose mind to choose to consume the more expensive service or buy the more expensive product. To answer this question. it depends on whether the consumer has an imperfect understanding of whose own tastes or the consumer has a perfect understanding of whose own tastes to the product or the service.

It means the consumer will choose to buy the product or consume the service, even it's price is higher than other general similar products or services if who has a perfect understanding of whose own tastes to the product or service. Otherwise, who won't choose to buy the product or consume the service, due to it's price is higher than other general similar products or services if who has an imperfect understanding of whose own tastes to the product or service. So, it seems that the consumer's negative or positive emotion arise will be influenced by whose perfect or imperfect understanding of whose own tastes to the product or service factor.

It concludes that whether how much degree of the consumer's utility to the product or service. It is not the only one important factor to influence the consumer to choose to buy the product or consume the service. Otherwise, the consumer's imperfect or perfect understanding own tastes to the product or service factor will influence the consumer to arise positive or negative emotion to make final purchase or consumption decision immediately. It will be one more consumption influential factor to lead the consumer to make the final consumption decision making immediately. So, future (AI) tool ought to be innovate to own how to judge good taste or bad taste for any food in order to predict food consumers to choose to buy the food manufacturer's any foods more attractively.

Chapter Two
(AI) tool technical innovation in cruise tourism
immediate positive emotion influence to
cruise travelling consumers

Can apply (AI) tool to cause positive emotion to cruise tourism consumers? Cruise tourism industry is the most influential emotion industry example to influence cruise travelling consumers' travelling entertainment choice. I shall indicate some evidences how it's innovation will influence cruise travelling consumers' emotion to be changed to positive from negative immediately as well as to prove how the cruise traveler higher utility feeling to the cruise tourism provider is not the main factor to influence whom to choose the cruise provider to consume whose cruise journey service arrangement.

Nowadays, cruising has become one of the fastest growing sectors within tourism, cruise service providers need have themselves unique different entertainment service arrangement to satisfy every cruise travelling consumer individual needs in order to attract every one to choose whose cruise arrangement easily, e.g. meals, activities, entertainment and varied destinations create one-stop holiday shop, reasonable competitive ticket fare. Hence, it seems it is one exciting emotion industry. If the cruise service provider can bring positive emotion to influence many cruise travelling consumers immediately. The, even it change higher service fare to compare other similar cruise service providers. I believe it won't influence them to choose other similar cruise service providers if it can often bring immediate positive emotion to its cruise clients during they are staying in its cruises or during they have left its cruises, but they will often remember or won't forget to enjoy their cruise service provider's happing time forever. Hence, if (AI) tool can be attempted to help cruise entertainment providers to arrange different cruise journeys for varied destinations , to arrange different entertainment facilities, to arrange the different taste food to satisfy different countries age cruise consumers' needs. Then, the (AI) tool will assist the cruise providers to bring positive emotion to let every different countries age cruise consumers to feel satisfactory in order to choose to the cruise providers' cruise entertainment service more attractively.

2.1 How can apply (AI) tool to predict cruise service providers bring positive emotion to their clients?

Future, (AI) tool can help any cruise providers to design these kinds of any one entertainment service arrangement to satisfy the cruise provider's customers' needs.

There are different special interests cruising , such as wellness at sea, freighter cruises, river cruises. It has increased the attractiveness of cruising: Romance is for lover cruise traveler target, luxury is for rich cruise traveler target, exotica is for enjoyment exciting feeling traveler target. So, every kind of cruise traveler target will have different kind of cruise entertainment service to satisfy their needs. If the cruise service provider can provide the right and attractive cruise entertainment service to satisfy the specific cruise target. Then, it will bring the positive emotion to the specific cruise target consumers more easily.

Cruise travel was shaped for mass tourism. Prices have been very differently segmented. There are basically four types of markets ( Biederman, 2008):

● Contemporary market: On board fun and amenities are playing important role and destinations have secondary importance.

● Premium market: This category is more expensive than the contemporary category and where the destination has same importance as on board amenities.

● Luxury market: It was once dominant type of cruise tourism, but now it has only a small portion of the industry. Generally, it is the most expensive cruise category and usually it takes longer than average cruise days.

● Adventure/exploration: It refers relatively long cruises with special and exotic places where the destination is the main purpose of the trip.

● European cruise travel: Duration takes more five days than worth

American travel duration. There is a tendency on European market during the years that duration of travel is getting shorter. This short demand of is explained with the strong demand of customers ( Hensen, 2003). Beside this, it is most likely that cruise companies try to convince tourists with short haul travels instead of long term cruise trips for more expenditure.

Thus, I believe that even, the cruise service provider charges higher ticket which won't influence cruise consumers who do not choose its entertainment service on its cruises. If it can arrange the attractive cruise entertainment facilities and destination journey arrangement, staying days arrangement to satisfy different specific cruise target market needs absolutely in order to bring whose emotion to be positive to it's service provision. Then, the cruise service provider will attract many potential cruise clients to choose its cruise service absolutely. Otherwise, if it only bring negative emotion to its cruise clients, it will not attract many potential cruise clients to choose it or loses its old cruise clients, even, its cruise ticket price is needed to decreased in order to raise competitive effort.

In conclusion, I believe that future (AI) tools need to learn how to bring cruise consumers to arise individual immediate or expected positive emotion, this positive emotion consideration is more important to compare to how to reduce cruise ticket price in order to attract cruise clients in global cruise competitive cruise industry.

2.2 Differentiation through the characteristics of cruising route method from (AI) tool route judgement

Future, (AI) tool can attempt to help any cruise entertainment service providers to judge how to design different route to attract different countries age cruise clients' choices to satisfy their cruise journey entertainment needs. The determinants of the cruising route's characteristics ( functional, social, and emotion) is important factor to influence the cruise service provider's success. Cruising product is no longer selected primarily for the cruising service, but for the content of cruising route. So, the cruising route will influence the cruise consumer individual emotion, because it is the main service need for every cruise consumer.

The approach called the " land sea cruising in product development" is increasingly becoming an area of interest, e.g. determining the direction of the effects of the individual cruising route characteristics on service value's perception , and providing an evaluation model of the route's perception , and indicating significance variables of attraction.

The questions that cruise planners need to know: How does each of the identified determinants affect the overall perceived value of the cruise route? How the overall perceived value of the cruise route affects customer behavior intentions?

Because different routes factor will influence cruise consumer individual emotion changing seriously. It means the ship has become only a tool, when the offered route whose attractiveness highly influences the impression of the guests has become crucial.

Consumer behavior in cruising segment includes all the activities and influences in the selection of the specific cruise route. There activities result in decisions and actions related to a defined price, selection and reselection of cruising company ( Cannot, Brink and Brijball, 2006).

2.3 How to apply (AI) tool to arrange cruise route planning have close relationship to influence cruise consumer emotion?

Firstly, use value of cruising routes is based on the subjective experience, and shows how individuals assess the route during, or immediately after sailing. It is affiliated with the benefits that cruising guest realize by choosing a route , and it is subjective because it depends on the individual assessment ( photo taken on the route for one guest presents just a family souvenir, and for professional photographers are embodied financial capital).

Secondly, the utilitarian value is also subjective-oriented and is tied on the point where the inner and us ability of cruising routes are compared with the sacrifice of the client ( money and time). Finally, the value is considered as the outcome of the comparison of scarifies and personal benefits, which is resulted in essentially utilitarian nature.

Hence, route design is the main value of cruising tourism and it is primarily determined and analyzed from the aspect of observed customers. Otherwise, the cruise is only one tool to be caught for the cruise passengers, whether the cruise can let whom to sleep comfortable , providing what kind of food to them to eat, what kind of entertainment facilities are provided to them to play, these issues are not more important to compare how to design route to bring them to travel to anywhere to enjoy in this cruise journey factor. Because how to design the route factor can bring each cruise passenger to influence them to feel either negative or positive emotion directly. The whole route journey planning is the most influential factor to influence the cruise passengers to feel whether they ought choose it's service again or not in the future.

(AI) tool judges the difference between utility factor and emotion to influence consumer decision making

In economic utility or immediate (expected) emotion aspects, whether which is more influential to excite consumption. To analyze whether it is economic utility or immediate ( expected) emotion more influential to excite consumption. It depends on the consumer individual consumption choice is in which situations. For example, if the industry's general consumer individual consumption decision is concentrate on emotion influential aspect, such as cruise entertainment industry, hospital care service industry, theme park entertainment industry, movie watching entertainment industry etc. Above all these industries have same nature, it is service. So, it seems that service industry's main influential factor is immediate ( expected) emotion influence, it is not economic utility influence. Otherwise, product sale industry's main influential factor is utility.

3.1 (AI) judges consumer utility factor

For this toy choice situation example, parent choose to buy one toy to give whose child to play. They usually considerate which kind of toy is attractive to their child whom like to play. In many different kinds of toys choice, if the child likes to choose the kind of toy to play. After the child's parents had purchased the kind of toy to let whose child to play one period time, e.g. six month. Then, when the child feel that who has need to buy another new toy to play, due to he/she feels bored to play this toy. So, it seems that the child feels this toy has less utility or it's utility is decreased. So, he/she expects whose parent can buy another new kind of toy to let whom to play. It also implies that it is not emotion factor to influence the child to feel boredom and unfunny to play this kind of old toy after six months. It is the product's utility factor which can not attract the child to play it any more. So, this old toy's utility is decreased when this child spends six months to play it. This toy's value is only six month utility to this child to play. Otherwise, if this kind of toy is bought by another parent. It is possible that the another child like to play this kind of toy one year or more. So, it's utility to another child is one year or more period. So, product's utility period is difference, it depends on how long time of the user's satisfactory time.

As this toy case, the child's decision will influence whose parent choose which kind of toy to buy to whom to play. Usually toy price is not difference too much. Parent won't consider when the toy price will be increase or will be decreased to influence their emotion to decide not to buy the toy immediately. So, when the child like to play the kind of toy, even the product's price is more than other kind of toys, and the parent feel it is possible that the kind of toy's price will be fallen down later. They will still choose to buy the kind of toy to let their child to play, they won't be influenced not to buy this kind product by later cheap price factor. So, immediate emotion is not the main factor to influence this parent does not choose buy this toy at this moment. Otherwise, utility factor will influence when the parent will buy another new kind of toy to provide to this child to play. If the child enjoy to play it only three months, after he/she will feel bore and he/she will tell whose parent to buy another new kind of toy to let whom play when the fourth month is beginning. So, it implies that if the kind of toy product can have more attractive utility time, then it can attract many parent to choose to buy it among different kind of toys. Thus, when this kind of toy's utility time is longer time. Then, it is possible that it can influence many parents choose to buy it's different style or design of similar kind of toys to let their children to play. In general, when many parents accept to buy this kind of different style or design of similar toys to give their children to play. Due to it's popular long time utility factor, it will influence children like to play it longer time to compare other kind of toys. Consequently, it will influence parents do not need often spend too much money to buy other kinds of toys to give their children to play. So, longer time utility factor to the product can attract many consumers to choose to buy the kind of product to compare lesser time utility factor to the product. Hence, it proves the explanation why utility factor is the main influential factor to influence the consumer choose to buy the product.

## 3.2 (AI) judgement tool of Medical care and utility case

Medical care is an input in producing health, it is subject to law of diminishing marginal productivity. Health yields utility to the consumer. It is subject to law of diminishing marginal utility. It bring this question: Does either the patient's emotion or the medical care service or medical care product utility which one can influence the patient's hospital choice more?

To answer this question: We need to know medical care is one kind of nursing care service in hospitals or clinics and medical care product is one kind of medical care product sale from merchants, e.g. medicine or medical equipment. So, in medical industry which has different kind of medical care services to provide to patients in hospitals or clinics as well as which has different kind of medical care products sale, e.g. medicine or wheelchairs, heart health measurement equipment etc. different medical care products in medical health industry.

In medical care aspect, it is one kind of any medical care service to patients from hospitals or clinics. So, medical care is an input in producing health service to patients from hospitals or clinics. When the patient is admitting to hospital or clinic, who needs to see doctor and the doctor need to give the right medicine to the patient to eat to ill whose illness. Even, if the doctor feels the patient whom needs to live hospital for one time period. Then, the hospital nurses must need to take care the patient during he/she is living in the hospital period. Consequently, if the patent can be health in short time, e.g. within one week leaving time, then he/she will be shortened time to leave the hospital in next weak. Otherwise, if the patent can not be health in short time, e.g. within on week, then he/she needs to live the hospital more than one week, even, one month, three months or more. So, the staying hospital time will influence the patent's emotion to feel whether the doctor's effort. If he/she needs to live the hospital long time, he/she will bring negative emotion to feel the doctor's medical effort is not good. The doctor's medical effort can not achieve or satisfy whose expected emotion during whose staying hospital time.

Thus, medical care is an input service in producing health, it is subject to law of diminishing marginal productivity. When the patient does not need to live the hospital longer time, the patient will feel more satisfactory to the hospital's doctor and nurses' care effort as well as the patient can give less money to spend the expenditure to live the hospital. So, the law of diminishing marginal health productivity will explain the hospital will shorten time to the staying days of the hospital to the patent as well as the patient's care expenditure will be decreased when he/she only needs to live to the hospital in short time. Otherwise, the patient needs to live longer time in the hospital, it means that the diminishing marginal health productivity to the hospital, the patient's staying hospital days will be increased and the patient's medical expenditure to the hospital will also be increased. It will bring negative emotion to patient and why this negative emotion factor will influence the patient would choose another hospital to live or find other doctors to see if he/she felt illness in future one day.

In medical care product aspect, health yields utility to the consumer. It is subject to law of diminishing marginal utility. Because patient needs to buy different kind of medical equipment to use or medicine to eat to attempt to cure whose illnesses. So, if the patent can choose the right medicine to eat from the doctor's recommendation or if the patent can choose the right medical equipment to use from the doctor's recommendation. When the patient buy less number of medicine to eat, then he/she can be health or when he/she buy the medical equipment to use, then he/she can be health. Then, he/she will spend less money to buy medicine to eat or medical equipment to use and he/she can be health in short time. Then, the medical consumer will feel the medicine or medical equipment has good utility to satisfy whose medical needs. So, good medicine and good medical equipment can only need short time and less money to let the medical patient to be health.

3.3 Immediate ( expected) emotion factor

As cruise entertainment case, every cruise journey must provide fixed stay days on the cruise to let every cruise passenger to play to every cruise journey. So, cruise passenger can not change or extend whose fixed stay day choice in every cruise journey, when they had caught the cruise to go to sea on the day. Is implies that cruise entertainment has none longer time utility factor which can influence each cruise passenger's choice to each different design of cruise journey arrangement.

If the cruise passenger feels very satisfactory and enjoyable to the last time of specific cruise journey arrangement, e.g. five days and four nights New Zealand and Australia cruise journey. Due to this cruise journey can bring positive emotion to let the cruise passenger to let whom feel that he/she can not forget or remember this happy cruise journey forever.

It is possible that this time happy five days and four nights New Zealand and Australia cruise journey will bring positive emotion to influence this cruise passenger to choose to find this cruise service provider to help whom to arrange this same cruise journey or another similar cruise journey again after one month, or three month, or six month or one year or more. Due to this cruse passenger felt this cruise service providers' cruise journey design arrangement can satisfy whose needs and it can achieve whose expected emotion to be positive. So, this cruise entertainment industry must be immediate ( expected) emotion influential factor more than time utility factor to influence the cruise consumer's cruise service provider and cruise journey choices.

In conclusion, it is not only utility factor can influence consumption decision. It is emotion factor can also influence consumption decision. It depends on situations whether the consumer is choosing to buy one product or consume one service. If the consumer is choosing to buy one product, how long time of the product's utility factor which will influence the consumer choose to buy which product. If the consumer feels the product can give longer utility time among other similar products, then he/she will have more chance to choose to buy the product. Otherwise, if the consumer feels the product can give lesser utility time among other similar products, then he/she will have less chance to choose to buy the product. If the consumer is choosing to consume one service, emotion factor will influence the consumer choose to find which service provider to consume the same service or similar service. If the service provider can provide excellent service to the consumer, then it will bring positive immediate or expected emotion to whom and it can attract the consumer to choose the service provider again. Otherwise, if the service provider can not provide excellent service to the consumer, then will bring negative immediate or expected emotion to whom and it can not attract the consumer to choose the service provider again.

Why and how (AI) judgement tool can judgement what utility factors are to influence consumer emotion

In emotion and utility both aspects, they include these situations. I shall explain how and why emotion and utility factors can influence consumption behaviors in these different situations as below:

(1) In the first situation is brand factor, the brand image, product quality, product knowledge , attitude and

(2) brand loyalty intangible factor will attract the consumer individual purchase.

For example, luxury

products, e.g. luxury fashion brands of clothing. Brands like Zara from Spain and H&M from Seweden began to produce catwalk-style fashion at low cost offering consumers of luxury fashion alternatives at low prices.

Nowadays, the luxury fashion sector is the fourth largest revenue generator in France, and one of the most remarkable sectors in Italy, Spain , the USA and the potential markets of China, Russia and India. The luxury industry has increased having a huge youth in demand. The luxury consumer have much choice in products, shopping channels and pricing of luxury products. It has possible relationship of age, gender, income and other demographic factors with purchasing intentions to influence the rational and emotional buying behavior regarding luxury fashion products.

(2) The second situation concerns the decision-making of make or female consumers are possible experience an emotional desires and cognitive (

reasoning) mind in purchasing choice process. Their emotion includes negative or positive buying emotion and mood management and cognitive process components include cognitive deliberation, planning buying with the exception regard for the future.

University had been using analysis of variances tests, male and female students were found significantly different with respect
affective process components including positive buying emotion, and mood management and cognitive process components include planning buying.

Significant differences were also found between the following product categories: shirts/sweaters, skirts, coats, underwear, accessories, shoes, electronic hardware, computer software, music , CD or DVDs, sports, memorabilia, health /beauty products and magazines/books for pleasure reading. No differences were found in regard to suits/business wear and entertainments.

The investigate proved that some products will have different emotion influence to cause female or male students whose final consumption decision to buy the kind of product. So, the difference od male and female students will have emotion influence to make purchase decision to buy the product in consuming choice process.

(3) The third situation concerns search advertising factor, e.g. online search to influence consumption behavior. Advertising is possible one method to persuade the consumer to choose to buy the product, even the consumer does not know the product exists. For example, proper cloth, a company based in New York, has a site on the social networking site Facebook.

Whenever the company posts a new photos of its clothes, all its face book " fans" automatically receive the information on their own face book pages. "We want to hear what our customers have to say." It seems online advertisement is a potential promotion method to promote any new attractive products to sell to let publicity to know to buy. Internet is one popular communication tool to be used by youth today. So, when one company can have one website to let any youth to find and enter to the website to discover any new things easily. It will cause many consumption chances to let online potential clients to attempt to choose any products to make purchase decision from online advertising tool easily.

How does the role of advertising influence the purchase decision process? Needs and motivations are the starting points of purchase decisions. In fact, advertising is a communication of photo image, sound image, and word advertisement image channel to persuade consumers to choose to buy the brand of product or consume the brand of service between the merchant and its consumers from television, radio, newspapers, magazine, movie etc. channels.

Why does advertisement influence consumer choice? For this case example, when one buyer waits until more information is gathered before making a decision. The time, two types of cost are involved. First, there are psychological opportunity costs experienced by consumers who are deprived of the product who need and are consequently in a state of psychological tension.

As time elapses, this psychological tension becomes more frustration. Second, buyers experience costs with the information-gathering efforts. They must invest time and energy to visit several retailers, seek out and read advertisements, or inquire for other opinions about the best product to buy.

These delayed decision costs considerably increase as time elapses. The buyer must seek information until it is felt that a search for additional information will bring about more costs than benefits. So, an advertisement is reaching a potential buyer when who is seeking information will have a greater impact, since the buyer is spending time and effort needed to seek out this information himself and he is less likely to find other competing and advertisements to obtain the additional information.

In general, buyers are generally more responsive to different brand advertisements, when they are seeking information on these brands. This is why the becomes a choice target for the advertiser provided the advertiser can identify and locate them. Thus, a client has interested and is in an information-gathering stage is asked.

Then, the advertiser takes advantage of the consumer's having identified him or herself to send a series of informative and persuasive messages or to send a salesperson who will try to conclude a sale. Thus, advertisement gives a chance to let consumers to gather information to choose the best product to buy or the most excellent service to consume.

What of situations do merchants need advertisements promotion? The short purchase cycle markets are characterized by routine purchase decision processes or by limited problem solving when a new brand is introduced on the market, e.g. coffee, bread , sugar, soft drinks, canned vegetables and household and beauty care products fall into this category. Another irregular purchase cycle markets are characterized by products that are purchased more or less regularly , e.g. cookies, cake mixes, wines, food products. Finally, long or unpredictable purchase cycle markets include all durable products, such as cars, household appliances and furniture ( products from which occasions of purchase can't be predicted, which most consumers buy only occasionally). Hence, these kinds of products ought need advertisement promotion specially, due to advertisement can build brand image to let consumers to know. Especially , it is a new brand of product. In conclusion, advertisement will be one good channel to let new product to introduce its brand to let clients to remember in minds heart.

Consequently, future (AI) tool needs to learn how to design different kinds of advertisement to attract consumer attention to the product, needs to learn how to find what the bad factor(S) which cause(S) many consumers do not choose to buy the product, needs to learn when the product price needs to be raised up or fallen down in order to bring consumers' positive emotion to choose to buy the product immediately. SO, if (AI) tool can be invented to own itself effort to design different kinds of methods to predict consumer behavior in order to bring their positive emotion to the product successfully, then the manufacturer can earn positive consumer emotion advantage from the (AI) tool assistance for long term benefit to its product.

# FOUR

# PSYCHOLOGICAL METHOD PREDICTS CONSUMER BEHAVIOR

Can apply economic models solve marketing changing challenges?

Economists indicate economic modeling can provide a logical, data to help organize the analyst's thoughts. The model helps the economist logically isolate and sort out complicated chains of cause and effect and influence between the numerous interacting elements in an economy. There are four types of models used in economic analysis: Visual models, mathematical models, empirical models and simulation models. Visual models are simply pictures of an abstract economy: graphs will lines and curves that tell an economic story. It is one kind of micro or macro-economic method to predict consumer behavioral change. Some visual models are diagrammatic such as which flow the income thought the economy from one sector to another ( micro economic environment). It is mathematical model, when it is presented the mathematics are explained what the data analysis is or not. The model does not normally require a knowledge of mathematics, but still allow the presentation of complex relationship between economic variable.

For example, the common supply-and demand model is meant to show the effect of inflationary expectations upon price and output. In this application, an increase in inflationary expectations causes demand to shift, raising prices and outputs (macro-economic environment). For another example, a very simple micro-economic model would include a supply function (explaining the behavior of products or those who supply commodities to the market), a demand curve ( explaining the behavior of purchasers) and an equilibrium equation, specifying the simple conditions that must be met if the model's equilibrium is to be satisfied. So, the variables in a model like this represent a type of economic activity (such as demand) or data ( information ) that either determines or is determined by that activity ( such as a price or interest rate variable change activity).

Dynamic models, in contrast, directly incorporate time into their structure. This is usually done in economic modeling by this mathematical systems of difference of differential equations. For example, it can use a difference equation from a business cycle model, investment now depends upon changes in income in the past. Time is incorporated into the model. Dynamic models, when they can be used, sometimes better represent the business cycles, because certainly behavioral response and timing strongly shape the character of a cycle.

For another example, if there is a delay between the time income is received and when it is spent. A model that can capture the delay is likely to those higher consumption desire to the consumer. It is a micro-personal behavioral consumption predict method. So, the user can experiment with an endless variety of values and assumptions to see whether results obtained are realistic or insightful. Since computers are now powerful and cheaper, the importance of dynamic simulation models should follow the future prediction time, when the consumer income receive and when it is spent to predict how much degree of the consumer's consumption desire in micro-economic view point.

Another model to be applied to predict consumption behavior. It is expectations and enhanced model, it includes one or more variables based upon economic expectations about future values. For example, if consumers for whatever reason, expect the inflation rate to be much higher next year, then this year, they are said to have formed inflationary expectations. If numerical values are being used in a model and the current inflation rate is 9%, if they expect inflation to be higher next year, the variable for inflationary expectations might be given be a value if 12% or more.

Normally, though general models used for instruction or analysis, it assumes an expectation value to be high. Where it will have an impact on the models result or " low" or " mot existent" where it will have no impact. In the simple supply - and demand to model presented earlier, inflationary expectations were high, shifting the equilibrium and causing higher prices and output. Hence, expectations and enhanced model as well as demand and supply model is a good predictive tool to predict when inflationary rate rises to the general unacceptable level to consumers to influence their consumption desires in societies in micro and macro-economic both view point.

What factors can reduce social consumption desire in general. The theory of rational expectations presumes that expectations are formed when economic agents see new developments in the economy and they logically deduce expectations based upon the information they have. For example, if the country's government central reserve system were to suddenly increase the money supply, according to the theory of rational expectations, consumers would immediately form inflationary expectations, not because prices are actually rising, but become they deduce that excessive money supply growth is likely to cause inflation. It presumes that a relatively high degree of raising consumption desire to people or people have access to, or even care about, information on the economy, such as the money supply growth rate, the rate of taxation etc. So, it's the government micro or macro-economic policy to attempt to raise consumption desire, due to people feel more money supply to society. So, it causes the feel salary increase. Due to money is excessive supply, so they will accept to consume more. But in fact, their salaries growth, it is due money supply growth. Moreover, due to the social businessmen had not raise products price to sell, e.g. food price, entertainment price, school fee etc. Different kinds of consumption price. So, it makes consumers feel their salaries growth and social consumption expenditure have no growth to influence them to feel they have more extra income to accept to buy any more things to consume in society. So, the government inflationary policy ( supply more money to society) is one example of macro-economic method to persuade people to accept more consumption behaviors in this inflationary ( increasing money supply to society) period. It aims to assist social businessmen have more consumption in order to avoid businesses failure risk in society.


1.2 Micro and macro-economic analysis methods solve Starbucks coffee shop faces marketing change challenges

This Starbucks case indicates how Starbucks coffee drinking business applies micro and macro-economic analysis methods to predict consumer behavior. Today, Starbucks has become world famous and brings high quality coffee and beverages to its clients over the world daily. Their well-known mission statements is: to inspire and nurture the human spirit, one person, one cup and one neighborhood at a time.

How does it apply macro and micro economic analysis methods to predict consumers' coffee taste more accurate? According to the following statistics, coffee market is large market potential in the world for this particular coffee service and production. Starbucks along with many competitors, such as Costa coffee and Mc-cafe have seized this opportunity and continue to indicate within this coffee market. It is no doubt that this coffee market can be profitable in 2012 year, the CEO of Starbucks was classified as the 8th best -paid CEO in the United States of America making $ 103 million dollars of profit ( Rushe, 2013). Hence, the question concerns that how Starbucks can predict its coffee customer fast accurate.

Micro and macro-economic marketing environment analysis: It is crucial to be aware and understand environment in which a company is operating in order to implement their strategies successfully. The micro environment strategies can be analyzed using in SWOT analysis and further completed with a macro environment study by doing a PEST analysis.

As Starbucks background, it can apply micro environment " a SWOT analysis" method, it must focus on the external factors since internal factors are rather analyzed in the core marketing strategy and extended marketing strategy and extended marketing mix. However, macro environment refers to everything external to the organization. So, it seems Starbucks can't necessarily fully control, only influence. Such as PEST analysis indicates political, economic, social and technological external environment factors. Such as certain political issues can raise since coffee beans are grown in developing countries and this could raise questions about the working conditions and child labor. Tariffs and import taxes could also influence the prices in stores as well as the country's economic recession or exchange rates change could threaten Starbuck's profits.

However, Starbucks internal strengths include that the development of new technologies and user friendly machines, such as home coffee machines, quality of beverages in other restaurants served are increasing and Starbucks should create Starbucks experience at home by manufacturing their own capsules machine with their coffee and tea. The emergence of social media is already used by Starbucks especially via Twitter where gift cards can be purchased and sent to friends ( Starbucks, 2014). There are Starbucks internal strengths to win its competitors, although, it can not control external environment factors to threaten its business.

Coffee drinking sale industry is a service marketing, positioning has received little attention from marketers, but is very useful in defining and modifying the tangible characteristics of the different kind of taste coffee product and its intangible perceptions.

As Starbucks, customers are buying an expensive product high quality (tangible ) every cup of different kind of taste coffee, but they also have the personalized in-store drinking experience enhanced by the trained employees, for example, the customer's name is written on the plastic cup their beverage will be served in ( tangible ), this helps Starbucks obtains the premium brand status and win competition.

Due to coffee drinking industry is a competitive business. In micro economy analysis strategy ( supply and demand). Nowadays, different coffee drinking service stores supply numbers are increasing. Although, it has limited supply numbers growth. Also, coffee drinkers' taste demand is changed quickly , who need to drink different kind of

good taste coffees and they also considerate coffee stores' staffs service performance when they can let them to feel enjoyable to sit down the coffee shops to drink its coffee. Hence, Starbuck considers its employees' service performance issue. It concentrates on training its staffs to let its every coffee drinking client has unforgettable drinking coffee enjoyable experience in its any one coffee shop. It implies Starbucks employees' service behavioral performance can influence every coffee drinkers' positive or negative emotion to decide to choose to go to Starbuck to drink coffee again or choose another coffee shops to drink coffee. Hence, Starbucks employees' service behaviors must have relationship to influence its future coffee drinking client growth number. If it's employees can provide kindly service attitude to every coffee drinker, adds it can produce any kinds of good taste coffees, adds it can let coffee drinkers to feel it's every cup of coffee price is reasonable. Sum of all the factors, they can influence why Starbucks can earn more sale of its coffee shops in global different countries in short term successfully.

I conclude that Starbucks still needs to find different kinds of new taste coffee to satisfy different coffee taste clients' needs. Because coffee drinking market will have many clients who like to drink different kinds of coffee. If Starbucks can not increase to provide different kinds of new taste coffee to satisfy client individual drinking new coffee taste demand. Otherwise, other coffee shops can provide new unique different kinds taste of coffees to satisfy their drinking new taste coffee demands. Then, due to Starbucks limited supply of new taste coffee factor, it will have possible to influence its competitive ability in this competitive coffee drinking market.

In conclusion, it needs to consider how many coffee supply number is not the main factor to influence its success. Otherwise, how much different kinds of coffee taste supply is the main factor to influence its success because coffee drinkers can either choose to go to supermarkets to buy different brands of coffee to drink at home or choose to go to other coffee ships to drink the kinds of coffee taste which Starbucks can not provide to them to drink. So, satisfying coffee clients' different kinds of coffee taste demand will be one main successful key to Starbucks, it is not how many coffee number supply ( enough coffee number supply) factor to influence its success. It needs to find different kinds of new taste coffee to let clients to know and to have more coffee choice to drink to satisfy their drinking new taste of coffee needs. It reflects the new taste of coffee supply and the new taste of coffee demand micro economic theory to influence coffee consumers' drinking behavioral needs in this coffee drinking industry.

Chapter Two

Micro economic assess the influence on location choices and growth performance consumption prediction.

Some economists indicate idea that seen central to the development of regional science at large and to economic geography and international trade theory. In this terms of economies of specialization increase returns to scale and in the case of regional science and economic geography, economies of localization and urbanization.

The questions concern: Can choose the best business location to attract consumption growth performance? Does the best destination attract consumption growth?

" Two cities attract trade from an intermediate town in the vicinity of the breaking point, approximately in direct proportion to the population of the two cities, and in inverse proportion to the squares of the distances of the intermediate town" ( Reggiani, 1998).

It implies some economists believe that geographic location choice factor can influence consumption growth. It is possible due to the location has many people are living. So, it brings many business chance, or the location is one the country's main in economic development location, it can attract many travelers choose to go to the location to travel. So, it has many travelling clients to prefer to consumer.

However, a smaller region can still attract consumption growth, if it had good transportation system. For example, a small region may not have its own university, but inhabitants may still have access to higher education. Elsewhere accessibility measures are also need in activity location models, where access ability is the way through which the quality of the transport system influences the land use.

So, it seems although the regional land is small size and far from cities, but if it can have good transportation system to provide any people to travel the small size regional land from outside cities. It is possible to bring consumption growth. However, some economists believe that distance influence relations in economics and economic geography in two ways: first, natural resources are distributed unevenly across space and second, distance separates various activities from each other. They apply " law of demand" to support their reasons.

In regional sciences, accessibility plays an important role for analyzing the distribution of economic cities and regional development. Within regional science, the attempt to predict and explain the distribution of economic activity has become known as economic geography. Research in economic geography attempt to answer the question: What forces cause geographic behavioral consumption? Some economists support the production function and into the interaction between transportation cost and plant level scale economies, this geographical factor will bring much geographical behavioral consumption. For example, accessibility of population is an indicator of market size for suppliers of products and services, whereas successful ability to GDP could be an indicator of the market size for suppliers of high level business services ( Spiekermannn and Wegener, 2007).

However, some economists argue that market potential is not necessarily the actual market. For example, since a person can't make the same purchase at two different locations. Hence, they believe that is one person has make purchase in one location far from whose home. Then, if he/she find another location which is close to whose home. The, he/she must not choose to buy the same purchase again, even he/she believe the seller's shop is close to whose home location. It implies that far location is not one factor to influence consumers to choose to buy the product if the consumer lines to buy the product. Even, the seller's shop is far away from whose home, he/she will still choose to drive whose car or catch transportation tool to go to the seller's shop to buy the product far away from whose home. Otherwise, if the consumer does not like the product, even the product seller's shop is close to whose home. Although he/she can walk to the shop to buy the product in short time. He/she won't choose to buy the product, due to who dislike the product. Hence, even close whose home, the seller product price is cheaper than the far away whose home, the another seller product price is higher than the similar or same product.

In conclusion, we have been downward trend of transportation costs of people, product and information to influence any geographical consumer behaviors. It implies that firms and people become less to restricted in their locational choices, it should lead to a greater homogeneity across regions. However, there are still great variation across geographical space in terms of incomes, cost of living, regional structure of production etc. different locational factors to influence regional consumption behavior in different countries.

2.1 Media economic methods to predict readers' behaviors in publishing industry

Media economics the application of economic theories, concepts and principles to study the macroeconomics and microeconomic aspects of most media consumption and industries, for academic lecturers, policymakers, and industry analysts. Media economics methods include how to apply variety of methodological approaches both qualitative and quantitative methods and statistical analysis, as well as studies using financial, historical and policy driven data.

Some economists define land, labor, and capital as the three factors of production and the major contributors to a nation's wealth. Can land, labor and capital be as three main factors of production any books, newspapers, magazines etc. reading products in publishing industry? Some economists believed price was determined by the costs of production, whereas marginal economists equated prices with the level of demand can be any books, magazines, newspapers etc. reading products prices is either determined by the cost of printing production or equated any one kind of these reading products with the level of reader' demand more.

The marginal economists contributed the basic analytic tools of demand and supply, consumer utility and the use of mathematics as analytical tools to develop microeconomics. Can apply the basic analytic tools of reader demand and the any one kind of these reading products supply and reading consumer individual reading need, utility and the use of mathematics as analytical tools to predict any kind of reading consumer numbers and reading interesting topic choice in media industry?

However, some economists also demonstrated that given a free market economy, such as in free publish industry, the factors of production ( land, labor and capital) were important in understanding the economic system. Can apply the factor of production , e.g. publishing book sale location ( land); publishing book salespeople sale experience ( labor); and attractive book printing quality (capital printing expense) to influence the publishing industry reading consumer reading habit or purchase book activities?

However, some economists suggested two important contributions: Analysis of monopoly and price discrimination and the market for labor will influence consumer number. Such as publishing case: Can analysis of which famous royalty publishing book sale firm to the most monopoly and then following its different topic of books sale price to evaluate whether how much every different topic of its similar book topic sale price to be higher to avoid reduce reader numbers, due to the not famous royalty book seller which similar topic book to the famous royalty book seller's prices are too higher than the famous royalty publishers' book prices?

Book salespeople individual sale experience and sale ability and book knowledge ( labor supply) influence the book publishing shop's reading clients buying decisions, such as the more experience book sellers can persuade many readers to buy the book store's books. Otherwise, the less sale experience book sellers can not persuade many readers to buy the store's books.

As the found in the field of economics, it became more refined, scholars began investigate many different economic concepts and principles to predict consumers behaviors, such as media reading customer. Nowadays, the media industries provides all of the elements required for studying the economic process. Content providers can offer information and entertainment, education etc. different topic books, magazine reading products which became the media publishing suppliers. Whereas, reading consumers and media advertisers formed the demand side of the media market.

The macroeconomic market conditions and the relationship among any media publishing reading product suppliers in various industries created microeconomic market conditions , e.g. publishing suppliers need logistic transportation service suppliers to help them to deliver books or magazines or newspapers etc. different kinds of reading products to book shops or magazine shops to sell every day. It can bring the logistic transportation service business to contribute social economic development.

Early media economists apply microeconomic concepts to examine newspaper competition and radio competition media industry. They predicted advertisement can help these both media industry to earn advertisement income to help other businesses to promote their products to let radio listeners and newspapers readers to know from these two media channel effectively. So, they believed that newspapers and radio extra income source can be provided advertisement service for other businesses, instead of radio audience income or newspapers reader normal income source. In addition to a number of book and edited volumes have contributed to the development of media economics to help them to predict consumer reading psychology.

How to apply media economic methods to predict media consumer's psychology? Some media economists believe the market structure-conduct performance model is as a tool for analysis, it has been widely used in the study of media markets and industries, such as book publishing industry. How to choose the attractive topic for every book product structure? They believe attractive book structure will help book structure firm to grow reader numbers. So, book topic and content factor is more influential to raise reader number more than cheaper book price sale factor.

In its most simply for the industries organizational model indicates that of the structure of the market is known, it allows explanation of the likely conduct and performance among firms. For example, in terms of market structure, the variables used for analysis include the numbers of sellers/buyers, e.g. US publishing book market number of US book reading publishers/number of US book publishing sellers every year in US book publishing market; product differentiation, e.g. US different topic and content of electronic book or paper book product ; barriers to entry, e.g. economic recession, tariff book import tax, limitation of import book number etc. different external barriers factors to influence overseas ( foreign) book publishing import to US to sell their paper books ; cost structures, e.g. US book publishing firms need to spend how much printing expenditure to print high quality paper production of every paper book to sell and the degree of vertical integration, e.g. US book publishing firms how to choose middlemen to help them to sell books, e.g. themselves book publishing shops, other book retailers, themselves electronic book publishing website online platform sale channel or other book publishing sellers' websites online platform sale channel etc. different channels to sell the paper of electronic books to US readers. Hence, predicting the country' book market structure, it will have more confidence to evaluate book publishing competitors' effort and book sale price and how to design book content and topic to raise reading quality to let readers to feel much attractive to choose to buy the books from the book publishing shop.

Media economics research is in the sense that many different types of methods are used to answer research questions and investigate hypotheses. However, many economists accept to choose to apply any one of methods to predict media reader behavior, such as trend studies, financial analysis, econometrics and case studies.

Trend studies compare and contrast data over a time series. In assessing media concentration. Most trend studies use annual data as the unit of analysis. Trend studies are useful, due to their descriptive nature and ease of presentation and they aid in analyzing the performance of media companies and industries, e.g. study of changes in newspaper pricing and subscription costs.

Financial analysis is another common methodological tool used in media economics research. Financial analysis can take many different forms and use different types of data. The most common data include information derived from financial statements and the use of various types of financial ratio.

Econometrics involves the use of statistical and mathematical models to verify and develop economic research questions, hypotheses and theory.

Case studies represent another useful method in media economics research. Case studies are popular because they allow a researcher to gather different types of data as well as different methods. Case studies in media economics research tend to be very targeted and focused examinations.

What are forces to influence media industry development? There four forces consist of technology, regulation, globalization and sociocultural can influence media industry development. I shall indicate why these forces will influence media industry change in order media industry businesses need to consider s below:

Technology force: Because media industries are heavily dependent on technology for the creation, distribution and exhibition of various forms of media contents, changes in technology affect economic processes between and within the media industries. For example, many publishing book businesses choose to apply internet technology to help authors to publish electronic books sale. Due to it is popular to let online readers to study from internet, even they choose to pay visa card to buy electronic or paper books to read from internet sale channel. So, technology brings electronic book digital content and text and graphics digitally soon led to digital audio and video files to let authors to download their files to change to electronic books to publish to sell to electronic book readers to read from online channel. So, internet builds electronic book web sites to attract reading consumers to read from internet channel. They do not need to bring paper book to read. They only need to bring mobile phone or laptops to go to anywhere to read electronic books any time conveniently.

Regulation: If regulation is eliminated in publishing or media industry to any countries, the cross ownership rules would give publishing companies. The opportunity to acquire broadcast stations able cable systems within the markets, they serve, leading to the development of multi-media based companies offering content and advertising across multiple mediums.

Globalization can influence media industry development. Media products are often created with global audiences in mind, which is why so much content contains sex and violence. However, globalization of media content began with motion pictures and magazines, but then expanded into another media channels, e.g. television programming, VHS and DVD sales and rentals. These media publishing products' income are influenced by global audience entertainment choice.

Finally, it is socio-cultural force factor which can influence reader or media entertainment consumer industrial consumption behavior. Socio-cultural, such as the country's young people accept to like to read electronic books more than paper books reading behaviors. Then, it is the country's socio-cultural factor to influence the country's book buyers who prefer to pay visa card to buy electronic books to read from book store online website platform channel. It is electronic book reading cultural trend to influence the country young people reading behavior change . They will change their traditional reading habits to choose to buy electronic books to read from internet reading channel. So, online reading of electronic book method will be popular to the country and the country's paper book publishing shops ought consider to apply internet technology to develop their electronic book publishing business to let young people electronic book buyers to read electronic books from online channel conveniently.

Finally, all media industry players ought consider any technology development in order to predict readers' or media entertainment players' whose consumption behavior changes to avoid themselves publishing media businesses encounter fail in future one day.

Can predict the real economic situation using liquidity of financial assets?

How about alternative ways of measuring liquidity? Can liquidity predict turning points of a business cycles or predict whether customer number will grow or reduce in next year? Is it a good consumer number predictive tool for alternative macroeconomic predictive results? Can liquidity predict real economy variables in macro-economic view point, i.e. such macro-economic aggregate ass economic growth ( changes in GDP), investments direction changes etc.?

There are some analysis to support its possibility , such as: Most of the predictability is coming from changes in the liquidity of small stocks ( presumably the least liquid ones). How about alternative ways of measuring liquidity? IS it real liquidity? If so, which aspect concerns to the liquidity to the company? So, the conclusion of question concern: Can liquidity method predict macroeconomic variable?

Consumer changing expectation to consume any things will be possible to influence macroeconomic variable. If it is true, calculating how many of the kind of businesses liquidity data that can predict whether the year macroeconomic variable is better or worse to compare last year. Can it use the current and past year kind of businesses liquidity data to predict next year macroeconomic variable situation whether it is suitable

to any businessmen choose to do the kind of business or not to do next year. The resulting trading decisions reflects changing expectations about whether business cycles and consumers' taste or consumption desires whether they are changing or not to cause the kind of most businesses choose to liquidity finally. So, if one foresees a deteriorating economy , one wants to shift the portfolio into assets better predicted in that case. For example, when one foresee an upturn one will shift into materials as the demand for that industry's products is likely to be high when investments are increasing. Using the sector as explanatory variable, one may catch this kind of behavior, since order flow is increasing in the desire for that particular sector.

So, if liquidity of asset method can be attempted to predict whether next year which kind of businesses will have risk. Then, it brings these questions: Which liquidity measures are the best for forecasting?

How does liquidity measures relate to alternative forecasting variables?

I shall assumes that it has relationship between stock market liquidity and cost of trading shares, with macroeconomic conditions. For example is that liquidity levels of local stocks are higher ( lower) , when the local economy has performed well ( poorly). The relation is stronger when local financing constraints are more binding, the local information environment is more better or worse, and local businessmen ownership levels and trading intensity are higher. More liquidity seems temporary relationship, due to short time economic recession factor to influence some kind of businesses , but still, linking the country local stock liquidity with local business cycle, it is possible that the country's different kinds of businesses will liquidate more than one year if the country's economy is recession long time. So, predicting many kind different kind of businesses liquidity choice in the country in the year. It will predict how long time the country economic recession will occur or find what factors cause the country economic recession occurrence in possible.

In conclusion, it seems that gathering the country's any kind of businesses whose past liquidity of financial assets data, it will possible to predict whether what kind(s) of businesses has( have) risk to do the kind of businesses next year. What factor(s) cause(s) the country's economic recession, economic recession situation will remain how long time, This liquidity of financial assets data gathering method will give opinions to let the country's businessmen to choose whether it is right time to set up their new businesses next year or close down their old businesses to be better next year.

3.1 Micro solution methods solve macro-economic problem

Nowadays, global financial crisis cause a slowdown in world trade growth. The recent great recession has important impacts on international trade. The international trade has changed from three factors: The evolution of global imbalances, trends in globalization and the structure of trade negotiations.

For example, new technologies in manufacturing, connectivity and energy efficiency in particular, have the potential to transform the global economic risk. From macroeconomic perspective these new technologies increase potential growth, allowing the economy to grow faster and it may also put downward pressure on energy price. The US seems as a likely beneficiary, where its competitive advantage in the production and deployment of information technology is widely recognized. Otherwise, some countries' development could be threatened by the substitution of cheaper and more efficient capital for ( labor and by the shortening of global supply chains).

I believe new technologies have the potential to solve global macro economic development challenges from micro economic ( every country technological firms cooperation development) method. The reason as below:
(1) Recent advances in information and communications technology new innovations in methods of manufacturing and fresh ways of exploiting energy could bring significant growth benefits for the world global economic technological development from different countries themselves technological firms research new ( undiscovered) technological products development to influence future human life, water energy, solar energy, nuclear energy, vehicle battery energy new energy development technology. It aims to avoid global energy shortage challenge occurrence and new artificial intelligent cities development, it aims to let human feel to live in high technological development, artificial intelligent cities can let human to live more comfortable and more convenient in global cities from artificial intelligent assistance.

For another example, some of the new technologies allow companies earn higher quality of physical capital at lower prices. Enhanced energy storage, shale gas and oil techniques, and innovations in renewable energy are helping to drive down the price of energy relative to the trend that would have unfolded in their absence. In all cases, new energy development, these technologies have the potential to raise productivity growth sectors and countries, allowing faster, new energy supply growth and lower inflation, when human have different kind of energy to choose to use.

For another example, mobile communications technology can make the world economy more efficient and may also lead to significant dislocation. Mobile communications technology has the potential to bring 2 to 3 billion people into the world economy development. Additive manufacturing as 3 D printing, could remove up to 90% of the waste from some manufacturing processes. At the same time, advanced robots which can work as little as USD$4 per hour, may eventually display existing employment in manufacturing. So, on micro economic view point, technology will be one kind production of factor to global future manufacturing firms. Mckinsey Global Institute finds that our trend global growth could be 0.5 to 0.7 percentage points higher in 2025s than in the absence of technological change, it implies productivity gains comparable to apply only personal computer and internet revolutions of the 1990s.

(2) What is future these new technology? A new technology ought change the way the world economy operates in micro economic view point. A new

technological change can shift the global economy's production function simply put, better technology allows the economy to produce more products and services at low prices. (production of factor). For example, potential efficiency gains include the widespread diffusion of mobile devices, easing access to the internet, artificial intelligence machine learning and voice recognition as well as the " internet of things", big of data gathering method to be applied to manage supply chains better in any factories ( production of factor).

(3) In manufacturing efficiency gains include the deployment of more advanced robotics making it more practice and profitable to substitute capital for human labor. Low-cost robots can change manufacturing by increasing precision and productivity without higher costs. Further efficiencies can be exploited with the use of 3 D printing, which reduces waste in manufacturing, improves precision of design and shortens complex supply chains ( production of factor).

(4) Finally, energy efficiency opportunities range from the extraction of oil and gas reserves from shale rock formations to enhanced energy storage. US storage team's work suggests that shale extraction techniques alone may add o.5% points per year to US growth over the next 10 years ( production of factor). New technologies may also put downward pressure on energy prices. Many of these technologies, such as waste -reducing , 3D printing, lower the energy intensity of global manufacturing and trade. By bringing product design and manufacturing closer to the end user, thus shortening supply chains, 3 D printing also reduces transport costs. The US department of energy anticipates that 3 D printing could save more than 50% of energy use compared to today's existing manufacturing.

(5) What new technologies influence global economy. Some economists predict new technologies will bring benefits to global economy development. They have conducted model simulations suggesting that global GDP growth could be 0.5 to 0.7 percentage points per annum higher as a result of the adoption and diffusion of these new technologies. the models also suggest that global inflation levels could be one percentage point lower than would otherwise have been the case.

However new technology can also bring some countries; labor marker change. Labor markets in manufacturing could be materially affected as capital in the form of robotics and 3D printing replace low and semi-skilled jobs. For some new technological global manufacturing and trading system countries. For example, in South Asia, the Middle East, Africa and parts of

Latin America development could be threatened by the shortening of global supply chains and by the substitution of cheaper and more efficient capital for labor.

Hence new technological manufacturing development will bring disadvantages to these without effort development of new technological manufacturing and trading system countries to influence themselves labor unemployment, if their employers choose to buy other countries' new technological manufacturing system, e.g. robots replace the human labor to help them to manufacture their products. Hence, it seems new manufacturing technology will have negative impact to the without effort development new technological manufacturing countries' manufacturing labor. Due to the robots can raise productivities to shorten manufacturing time and no salary expenditure and robots efficiency is higher than human labor.

However, if these countries' labor can learn how to apply robots knowledge to control robots to help their employer to manufacture products. It is possible that they won't be dismiss, even employers will need them to assist them to control the new robots manufacturing machines to manufacture their products in factories. It depends on whether they choose to attempt to control manufacturing robots or not.

In conclusion, new technology can be one important production factor to influence global macro-economic growth from micro new technological manufacturing sectors development. So global manufacturers will concern how to apply new technology to help them to manufacture any products.

3.2 Economic science or economic art methods predict consumer behavior

Economic is both a science and art. Economic is considered as science because systematic knowledge derived from observation, study and experimentation. An art is the practical application of knowledge for achieving definition ends. A science teaches us to know a phenomenon and art traches us to do a thing.

How to apply economic science or art method to predict consumer behavior? for example, there is a inflation US this year. This information is derived from positive science. The government takes certain fiscal and monetary measures to bring down to general level of prices in the country. The study of the monetary measures to bring down inflation makes the subject of economics as an art. Hence, as this case, if US government applies economic science or art method to predict this year will have inflation in US, then US government will attempt to avoid social general product prices to be raised, due to inflation influence. It aims to avoid US consumers reduce consumption desire in this year.

For another example, nothing could be more useful than water. But in much of the world waste is plentiful enough that another glass more or less matters little to a fresh water supply agent businessman. So, water is chap. But, if any offices buy bottle of glass fresh water to let employees to drink. It will bring advantages that they do not spend time to buy water to drink when they are working in the office time in any offices as well as employees do not need to heat water to drink to waste time to work in offices. So, the bottle of fresh drinking water supply agent is one kind of drinking water product monopoly fresh drinking water supplier to supply fresh drinking water to satisfy office employees who do not need to spend time to heat water to drink in offices. Hence, it is possible that replace other different kind taste of drink or office employees themselves heat water drink in offices. It is general office employees' drinking habits and drinking choice in offices popularly. So, the bottle of fresh drinking water supply agents will concentrate on selling their fresh drinking water to office employee customers only in global fresh drinking water consumption target market. The office employees must be fresh drinking water companies' main target consumers.

What is economic laws qualitative or quantitative method to predict consumer behavior? Law of economic are qualitative in nature. They are not exactly stated in quantitative terms. They tell the direction of change which is expected rather than the amount of change. For example, according to the law of consumer demand, the quantity demanded varies inversely with price, We don't say that 10% rise in price will lead to 30% fall in the customers' quantity demand.

What is economic merits of deduction method? This method is near to reality. It is less time consuming and less expensive. the use of mathematical techniques in deducing theories of economics brings exactness and clarity in economic analysis. The deductive method is highly abstract. It require a great deal of care to avoid bad logic or faulty economic reasoning. This method makes conclusions to predict consumer behavior, due to reliance on imperfect and correct assumptions.

It involves the process of reasoning from particular facts to general principle on the basic of experimentations, observations and statistical methods. In this method, data is collected about a certain economic phenomenon. There are systematically arranged and the general conclusions are drawn from them.

What are the advantages of inductive method to predict consumer behavior? It is based on facts as such the method is realistic. In order to test the economic principles, method makes statistical techniques. The inductive method is therefore more reliable, inductive method is dynamic. The changing economic phenomenon are analyzed and on the conclusions and solutions are drawn from them and this method also helps in future consumer behavioral investigations.

However, inductive method has weaknesses to predict consumer behavior, such as below:

It conclusions drawn from insufficient data, the generalizations obtained may be faulty. The collection of data itself is not easy task. The sources and methods employed in the collection of data differ from investigator to investigation. The result, therefore may differ even with the same problem and it is time-consuming and expensive to find data to predict consumer behavior changes.

How apply this method to predict general social consumer sources of income and consumption pattern when economic environment factor changes consumer behaviors? It should also be stressed that micro analysis plays other roles. First, it may serve to some macro data (any labor force by production sector or by skill category). Second, it can be used to estimate of key consumer behavioral consumption functions. For example, price and income elasticities can be estimated using data available in a typical householder budget survey. Third, in the case of tax reforms involving changes in exemptions or deductions is a model useful to estimate changes in effective tax rates changes how to influence consumer behavioral changes in society.

In conclusion, economists have proved macro and micro economic both methods have possible to be applied to predict consumer behavior when , how and why their consumption behavioral changing occurrence in order to manufacturers and product sellers or service providers can pre-make judgement to achieve the marketing strategies to avoid the number of client loss, due to marketing or economic environment changes to influence negative impact to consumer behavioral changes to influence the manufacturers' manufacturing products or the sellers' products or the service providers' service provision which number to be decreased.

# FIVE

## MARKETING COMMUNICATION STRATEGY PREDICTS CONSUMER BEHAVIORS

What are marketing communication
strategy benefits?

Can marketing communication strategy help organizations to build brands, innovation, developing relationship, create good consumer service and communication benefit. Most marketing professionals believe effective communicaton strategy can help organizations to raise brand competition as well as to create and enhance relationship with consumers and other stakeholders. Marketing communication strategy is concept of communication through the promotional mix, with these better-educated, cost-conscious and demanding customers.

Why do organizations need marketing communication strategies? Marketing communication strategy is concept used for sales promotion, product publicity, events sponsorships and direct marketing. It can help new brands to raise familiarity to let customers to know when the brand product plans to enter the marketing to sell in beginning.

Nowadays, organizations need promotional mix strategy to let consumers to familiar their new products, such as public relations, marketing, advertising, promotion and online media. Generally, organizations expect to achieve these aims. Otherwise, one effective marketing communication strategy can assist the organizations to drive forces for growth.

The driving forces include: Value of money means the organizations want to gain maximum value for money with maximum impact, resulting in raising value of money to different products in different departments and pressure on margains: Increasing pressure on organizations' bottom lines means organizations seek compensatory savings in all activities through saving, economic pressures and profitability, increasing client confidence means specially to understand retailers, cutomers and an increased confidence in using other marketing communication disciplines, a dissatisfaction with advertising means resulting in clients using other disciplines to improve consumer relations and sales, increasing mass media costs means where database costs decreased, mass-media costs ( especially television, increased dramatically) and a reduction advertising agencies expenses in terms of strategic input and direction. Hence, one effective marketing communication strategy can be possible to assist the organizations to reduce advertising expense, raise brand familiarity, increase client number, raise product sale price for long term benefits.

Some marketing professional researches recommend marketing communication strategy ought have these several stages, they include as below:

Stage one is tactical coordination of marketing communication. It means to find what are the fails on function areas including advertising, promotion, direct response, public relation and special events. The tactical coordination of marketing communication strategy aims to find why a high degree of personal and cross-functional communications needed as formal policies and procedures are insufficient to achieve the organization marketing communication operation. It aims to find what the weaknesses are to cause the organization's internal communication between different departments and external communication to its clients inefficiency and ineffectiveness.

Stage two is refining the scope of marketing communication. The organization begins to examine communication from the consumer's viewpoint, include all contact and entry points between the organization and clients. The scope of communication activities also include internal marketing to employees, suppliers and other business partners.

The extensive information on consumers is gathered through primary and secondary market research as well as actual consumer behavior data and feedback channels are created to gather information about consumers. So, it aims to find what marketing communication challenges influence the organizations' internal and external communication difficulties to influence poor unsatisfactory customer behavior performance to seek valuable solution to raise the organization's internal and external marketing communication more efficient and effective to raise customer communication success.

Then, third stage concerns how to improve and apply skill to build good marketing communication channel. Due to the marketing communication strategy implementation organization will need to learn how to use data obtained through IT skill to provide a basis for the identification of values and to monitor the impact of integrated internal and external marketing communication program over time. So, IT must be incorporated effectively into communication planning development and execution.

The final stage is financial and marketing communication strategic integration. It emphasizes shifts from skills and data to driving corporate strategic planning using consumer information and insight. Financial measures should be adapted into the evaluation process based on return on consumer investment measures.

So, these stages will be the key component to raise or improve the external marketing communication efforts with the internal marketing communication efforts to raise the overall organizational corporate brand for long term effective and internal and external marketing communication channels to employees and consumers both stakeholders' benefits.

## 4.2 Marketing communication functions

Why do organizations need marketing communication? What are marketing communication functions to organizations? What kinds of challenges will encounter if the organization lacked an efficient marketing communication strategy? This chapter will be explained above these questions clearly.

Marketing communication seems to be gathered information and communication seems to be gathered information and communication technology, which will influence every aspect of consumer need in order to bring positive or negative emotions to the brand of product. Hence, if the organization had effective marketing communication tools and strategies, which will raise its competitive effort in nowadays business societies.

An effective marketing communication strategy or tool will help the brand of product to build good emotion to its consumers. The steps include: The organization needs have one good marketing plan. Then, it needs to design the right or suitable kind of marketing strategy to satisfy its products or services characteristics. Finally, if its marketing communication tools or methods are suitable to the organization to be used to promote. Then, it will either build good brand or remember or familiar as well as build either good ( positive ) or bad ( negative ) emotion to the customers. So, it seems an efficient and marketing communication tool or method will help the organization to increase customer familiarity and build positive emotion to its product or service. Otherwise, an inefficient marketing communication tool or method will not help the organization to increase customer familiarity build negative emotion to its product or service. So, it is one important function to any marketing communication strategy.

Why organizations ought need to spend time and human resource / communication tool resources to design the most right or the most suitable marketing communication strategy for its organization to promote its product or service? Before any organizations design any communication strategy , they need to know what is this marketing situation. In general, marketing is defined the establishment of mutually satisfying exchange relationships between the brand's product or/and service and its clients. It is managing profitable client relationships. It's goal of marketing is to attract new clients by promising superior value and to keep and grow current clients by delivering satisfaction.

Therefore, the marketing function is to identify client needs and to provide a product or service that meets some or all of those needs, accessibily and at an acceptable price to the target market. Hence, the organization's marketing communication strategy is only one part of its overall marketing strategy. A marketing strategy includes how to help the organization to promote its product or service, how to sell its product or provide its service, how to arrange the reasonable price strategy, how to help the organization to improve production and distribution efficiencies, how to focus on continue product improvement, how to focus on aggregative selling tactics, focuses on customer needs, applied on integrated marketing approach, how to give welfare of society.

How does the marketing communication strategy influence the overall marketing strategy success to the organization? An effective marketing communication strategy can create value for customers and build good customer relationship for the brand of product or service. It's function includes that is can let the organization understands market places and its customer needs and want more clearly, it can assist the organization how to design a customer-driven marketing strategy if the organization can build good relationship between them , it can also help the organization to construct a marketing communication strategy( program) that delivers superior value. Then, when the organization has an efficient marketing communication strategy, it can help the organization to build relationship and create customer delight in long term. Finally, it can help the organization to achieve a superior capture value from its clients to create profits and client quality more easily.

Why do organizations need have an efficient marketing communication strategy? The reasons include that as below:

In fact, customers have much choices, usually different product or service marketing places will have ( excess) oversupply of product or service to influence consumers to make careful choices to buy which brand of product or consume service in whose choice processes. So, if the brand of product or service cn build good communication relationship between itself and customers. It can influence customers to have positive emotion to choose to buy its product or consume its service. So, any organizations needs have good price, location ( place), people ( staff) strategies, it also need have good promotion (communication) strategy in order to learn how to communicate to its customers to keep close relationship and build positive emotion to let them to feel.

However, the marketing communication must include these several tools for any organizations to choose which kind(s) of communication tool(s) is (are) the best tool(s) in order to be used to promote its clients efficiently. They include: Advertising, it means that controlled paid for communication, it consists of communication messages, initiated by a specific communicator in the mass media to a defined target audience. Personal selling involves interpersonal communication between sellers and buyers through personal interactions. Sales promotion concerns the free and favorable exposure of a product's benefits or value in the media, public relations can establish and maintain favorable relations between an entity and its stakeholders. So, any organization needs to choose either only use one kind of communication tool or more than one kind of communication tools in order to achieve an efficient marketing communication strategy to build positive emotion and good product or service image or familiar brand to let its potential customers to know by any above one media. Also, it implies that customers won't know or familiar to the brand more clearly if the organization had not implement any promotion tool(s) to promote its product or service to let clients to know whether its existing product or service can give what benefits to them.

How to achieve an efficient marketing communication strategy? To achieve an efficient marketing communication strategy to the organization. It includes this process: It needs to identify who are its target customers ( main target customer) potential customer and prospects. Then, it needs to measure the valuation of its different groups of client ( e.g. age, sex, shopping characteristics). Next, it needs to create and deliver the right or suitable or useful or persuasive messages and incentives to let its different group clients to know what its product or service existing in its country or global market places. Next, it needs to estimate how much it can earn return on its customer investment for its future possible reward. Because it if estimated that its marketing communication expenditure can not achieve its budget return in customer investment reward. Then, it needs revise its this ( these) kind of marketing communication tool (s) whether it ( they) is ( are) useful to promote its product or service to let clients to know. Finally, it needs to implement its budgeting allocation and evaluation to review its every time marketing communication tool(s) whether is (are) achieved its original aim. If it believed or confirmed its slae result is not successful. Then, it needs to revise its marketing communication tool(S) whether they (it) is (are) the most suitable or useful one tool(s) t be used to promote to its clients in the future. Hence, the whole process of marketing communication strategy is very important to influence its sale number. Every product or service provider needs to spend enough time and human resource to marketing communication tool resources to decide how to design to implement in order to sell in failure finally.

For one integrated marketing communication model of brand contact delivery system case example: The brands customer ( prospect exposure will include message and incentive both aspects. Message and incentive will bring promotion communication information concern relevance and receptivity to the brand's product or service to let its customers to know or remember or familiar by these any one or more than one delivery systems , such as product/use of the package product message tool or directed marketer channel or undirected member channel or traditional media tools ( accesses or unintentional , such as TV, radio, magazine, signage outdoor direct marketing tool or electronic media tools ( wired or wireless ) such as website second intranet or mobile phone engines GPS or special events promotion methods ( natural or sponsored) , such as holiday events or sport cultural trade events. All any one of these media delivery systems will be one choice tool to let the product/ service providers to be chosen to find which tool is the most efficient delivery tool. Hence, one marketing communication strategy elements include the marketing communication source is the company/brand or agency, the brand message concerns ( planned , unplanned, product or/and service) and the channel includes newspapers, TV, radio, magazine, e-mails, salespeople sale service, customer service, internet and the receiver is the target audience in the whole marketing communication process. Finally, the delivery system will bring feedback to the company/brand, agency and the target audience both. The feedback includes that purchase/not purchase, request information, visit store, sample product, repeat visit/purchase.

Consequently, any marketing communication strategy will bring feedback to let the product/service provider to know in order to judge or predict whether its potential customers will have positive or negative emotion ( attitude) to choose to buy its product or consume its service. Thus, feedback affect will be one important factor to influence the product or service providers success. If the product / service providers and clients both feedback trends to more negative emotion to its potential customers, then it can attempt to follow whose ideas to find what internet weaknesses or external threats to cause whose potential customers feel negative emotion to its product or/and service. Then, it can attempt to find solutions to avoid whose negative emotion is caused more easily. Thus, an efficient marketing communication strategy can help the product/service provider how to raise its potential clients' emotion to be trended more positive emotion for their product or service choices.

4.3 The possible sale of relationship marketing and communication in public utility service

What are the function of marketing communication to public utility service ? If the public utility service organization lacks an efficient communication channel between internal staffs and utility consumers, what kinds of challenges who will encounter. How to they make solution ? What are the negative attitude of the utility consumers will be if it lacked an efficient communication service between them?

In fact, many countries' public utility service is monopoly market. Their governments usually have a regulated prices to control their price to be charged to public utility consumers. Consumers have had affordable public utility access to these utility service, but they have been defense against the service providers . Hence , every government usually control utility service providers' price charged behavior in order to avoid their excess of charge. So, public utility service providers have realized that those is a competition on the utility service market.

Hence, an effective and efficient marketing communication channel will bring those benefits of advantages between the organization's internal staffs and every utility service consumer. I shall indicate the advantages as below: Firstly, an efficient marketing communication channel can let utility service consumers to feel whether the public utility service is a real public service. Due to public utility service aims to provide any enough utility remains to consumers to use, such as electricity , water, gas, oil etc. is the field on non-business marketing because the public utility service providers do need aim on profit seeking . This is made characteristics as well by the fact that in many service field, e.g. higher education, public transport, public utility service. So , an efficient communication marketing channel can let the public service consumersm who can make easy to distinct between public and private as well as between profit and non profit , e.g. the students can judge whether their schools charge higher education fee or lower education fee in the general school fee charge level and judge whether the public transport charges higher or lower transport for general public transport service standard charge level and judge whether the gas, oil, water, electricity utility service charge is accepted to general public utility service charge standard level. Hence, an efficient marketing communication channel can let the public service consumers have more familiar and effort to judge whether the public service providers' charge is reasonable.

However, an efficient communication marketing channel is very important to assist the public utility service consumers to make a distinction as well . Every public utility service organization has responsibility to let public service consumers to know what are basic services to be provided to let them to judge whether the kind of possibility of public service substitution is small or large to let the public service consumers to choose in the country 's current public service market to let them to judge whether the public service quality is good or bad and whether the price conditions are reasonable. Hence, an efficient marketing communication channel can build the good relationship between the public service organization and its public service consumers.

Do public utility services have important characteristics from marketing communication channel? It is agreed that efficient marketing communication channel is needed to any public utility service industries. It has chose marketing and communication relationship to any public utility service organizations. It is to think in terms of back office organizations in most person to person contact based services, but in the case of the utility services, the situation is unique different. In fact, the role of back office is significant different in the case of public utility services. In general , public utility consumers do not assess the work of background staff as they are unseen and are not usually part of the service providing process. However, the result of the servicing activity depends on the work of the back office. So, it explains that why efficient internal department communication is very important between public utility service back office staffs. There is no effective public utility service without the tools, equipment and operating staff and the application of efficient and effective communication relationship marketing is challenges by this fact. For example, the role of power , heating, water and long distance telephone supply etc. customer service front office staff role is influential to their service efficiency by the back office staffs cooperation. If they have good communication channel to let them to work in order to achieve efficient communication effect. Then, the front office public utility service staffs can provide better consumer service to satisfy any public utility service consumer needs or build the high direct consumer service relationships between them.

Besides, efficient communication marketing strategy can assist the public utility service organization to promote its prices to let public utility service consumers to feel more acceptable to the price level charge range. It is often difficult for service providers to apply differentiating price strategies and to use prices as promotional devices. Even, when price incentives are allowed public utility service providers rarely use. There effectively with elements of the marketing mix or with effective segmentation program to an efficient communication marketing strategy can help any public utility service organizations to solve any tangible and/or intangible communication challenges, such as back office and front office staffs communication challenges, fron toffice customer service staffs poor or inefficient service performance challenge, who causes utility service consumers to feel emotion unsatisfactory or do behavioral complains. So, effective communication marketing strategy is important tool to influence any public utility service organizations successes.

## 4.4 Understanding food industry marketing communication ( pull marketing communication strategy)

In food industry , it needs have an efficient marketing communication strategy in order to the food providers can persuade their food consumers to choose to buy their food easily. Firstly, the food provider needs to understand the global consumer's preference to find how any why to persuade they to choose to buy their food products. It is important to develop marketing communication strategies to solve challenges and find or seek opportunities in the communication process between the food providers (manufacturers) and its food retailers, food wholesalers ( supermarkets , food stores). In its communication marketing strategy, it needs to consider two channels: The first channel is supply chain development and management channel. The food supplier ( manufacturer) needs to learn how to manage its difference kinds of food supply chain, learn how to manage its food quality and food transportation logistics methods and learn how to communicate to its food retailers or food wholesalers how to help it to sell its different kinds of food to let consumers to buy attractively. The another channel is that it needs to learn how drive food consumer behavioral consumption and learn hoe to predict why whose consumption behavioral change. Hence, the food supplier ( manufacturer) needs to learn how to communicate with its food retailers and food wholesalers to know how any why its food consumers' choices to but its foods behavioral change. It concerns that it needs to communicate with them to learn how and why its old food consumers' taste change, research and builds new food product brand development as well as learns how to achieve efficient marketing communication strategy and point of sale strategies. Finally, the food supplier ) manufacturer) will gather all data from there both channels to brings all data together to implement strategy revisited and revised the weaknesses and keep strengths in order to find the most useful solvable method to attract new potential food consumers to choose to buy to food or keep its old consumers to continue to choose to buy its food. Hence, one efficient marketing communication strategy which can represent the " PROMOTION" element of the marketing mix. Such on this food industry case, food marketing is all about food selling and communicating ideas be they to buy a good taste of food or good food salespeople service or take notice of a public health appeal ( e.g. eat fruit and vegetable). None of this is possible without a good and effective communication strategy between the food supplier ( manufacturer) and its food retailers or food wholesalers.

In many food and agricultural markets, the food and agriculture suppliers ( producers and supply chain/ channel partners, it has become increasingly difficult to differentiate between food or agricultural product offerings. So, the number of available and positioning opportunities also diminishes. So, it implies that efficient communication strategy can assist them to create long-life marketing communication opportunities to promote their any agriculture food success. Some of the key roles that promotion can play in food marketing include as below:

An efficient communication marketing strategy can help the agricultural food producers to build brand depth awareness. For example, when some food consumers ask the supermarket staffs concern which brands of chicken taste that they can choose to buy in the supermarket chilled meat sections. If the chicken food supermarket staffs can speak some brands of chicken food, e.g. steggles, lillydale, ingham etc. brands. Then, the supermarket staffs can help those chicken brand producers to promote the different chicken taste food to let the supermarket consumers to know. So, it means that the brand of chicken food producers can build good communication relationship to the supermarket . Then, the supermarket staff's promotin behavior , it seems to advertise the chicken food producers to let the supermarket customers to know or be familiar the brand of chicken's different chicken tastes.

So, good food taste marketing communication strategy can achieve good or physical availability , such as the food producers can arrange how much different food distribution to different wholesalers or retailers, such as supermarkets, food stores. Hence, if they had good communication relationship, whose middle sale agents, such as supermarkets or food stores will tell about how much different kinds of food will encounter food shortage or food excess perishable challenges in next month in order the food producers can predict who ought continue to increase supply the kind of food or reduce supply for every kind of food to the supermarkets or food stores to help them to sell next month. It aims to achieve all food will be fresh and good quality to provide to food buyers to eat. So, predicting food supply number will be one important solution to food perishable challenge.

In conclusion, an efficient marketing communication strategy can assist the agricultural food producer to avoid to supply the excess of different kinds of food number or the shortage of different kinds of food number challenge. If the agricultural foods producers can build good marketing communication relationship between itself and its food wholesalers/ food retailers, e.g. supermarkets, food stores. Then, the food producers will have goods notice about its different kinds of food sale number data every month or every week ,even every day in order to decide whether it ought increase or decrease how much accurate predictive number of the kind of food to its food retailers or wholesalers to sell every day to avoid the different kinds of food excess or shortage challenges. So, efficient marketing communication strategy is very serious to agriculture food producers.

4.5 The role of marketing communication strategy in theatre management

Why does theatre industry need communication media, e.g. combination of advertisement, publicity, and public relation, plus other marketing tools in promotional activities of theatre management strategy. If the theatre performance provider neglected to achieve efficient marketing communication strategy , it will bring what kinds of challenges to influence performance entertainment consumers' entertainment desires.

Theatre industry can be explained to refer to any structure or group of people ( even non professional existing primarily for the preparation/ presentation of theatrical performance, such as dance, music, song, movie, life show etc. performance for purpose of audience entertainment activities, such as movie is one kind of popular entertainment in theatre industry. It can provide entertainment activity to entertain audience to satisfy their visible enjoyable desires when they had bought tickets to choose any movies to watch in theatres.

What is the purpose of communication marketing management principles and strategies to theatrical procedures? Theatrical communication marketing management strategy consists planning, staffing, organizing , motivating, directing and controlling human and material resources in the arts of the theatre and their interaction in order to attain the predetermined objectives of guaranteeing satisfaction and maximizing profit. So , theatrical organization needs have efficient communication between its internal departments as well as itself and its any performance entertainment service providers . It aims to achieve every final entertainment performances which can be more attractive to let audiences enjoy to watch or listen any kinds of entertainment performances.

What role is a directing communication channel to theatre industry? Advertising is the structured and composed non-personal communication of information usually paid for and usually persuasive in nature about products, services and ideas by identified sponsors through various media. Advertising can be explained the techniques and practices used to bring products , services , opinions or causes to public notice for the purpose of persuading the public to respond what is advertised. It seems theatre industry needs have efficient communication to let internal departments or entertainment performance service providers to communicate to them to achieve to prepare any attractive advertisement before any entertainment performance implementation. Because if one entertainment performance provider can provide attractive advertisements can persuade and notify potential audiences to choose to buy tickets to enter theatres to watch the entertainment performance service provider's any entertainment performance event more easily. So, the theatre service provider and its entertainment performance service providers need have good communication in order to advertise every different kind of entertainment performance event more attractive to let its audiences to feel. So, theatre provider needs to concern this internal and external communication issue in order to apply advertisement promotive channel to attract potential audiences.

Other kind of promotion channel to theatre providers. It is publicity , it is difference to public relations or even advertisement. Although, publicity seems a tool of public relations, but the aim of publicity is to create awareness through the media by placing news information about on organization, such as the theatre provider and its enteretainment performance service providers. The major characteristic of publicity that differentiates it from other marketing tools is tat it is not be paid for by an identified . Otherwise, public relation serves mainly the create an understanding between the theatre entertainment performance service provider and its publics ( audiences) , thereby creating awareness for its entertainment performances. A public relations campaign takes various forms. It can be through the theatre provider's sponsorship of program beneficial to the audiences or through the award of scholarships is through any music, song, movie, dance, life show etc. different kinds of entertainment performance projects that attempt to build better understanding between the theatre provider and its audiences . So, having taken a critical look of advertising , publicity and public relations will be the important part of communication or promotion tools in theatre industry.

The aim of every well communication methods to manage theatre , which can have much influential to impact audiences' emotions and their entertainment performance consumption desires to the theatre provider. However, the marketing communication channel of advertisement has weakness to theatre entertainment performance service provider, it depends on most printing spending times, as the printing of posters. This is not out of place because it has its role to play in marketing , but the fact, the electronic media advertisement does not need to print papers . Hence, this kind of promotion method will bring more economic benefit to the theatre service and entertainment performance service provider both.

A theatre entertainment performance provider will have different departments to cooperate efficiently in order to produces theatrical performances, such as drama, dance, movie, opera, music , life show etc. entertainment performances. So, one department of any theatre provider needs t make use of advertisement to create awareness about their any entertainment performance to any let audiences ( entertainment consumers )to know. So, efficient communication is necessary between the theatre provider's departments.

In conclusion, in theatre entertainment performance industry, any theatre entertainment performance providers expect their every movie, song, music, dance, life show etc. art performances can be promoted from advertisement , publicity and public relations marketing tools successfully. In efficient marketing communication strategy is an essential facility available to every internal departments in order to strengthened cooperation how to design every advertisement, publicity and public relations channel to let every different kinds of art performance to be promoted to attract potential audiences to choose to admission tickets to watch or listen the theatre entertainment performances more easily.

4.6 Marketing communication function in clothing industry

What marketing communication tools are the most useful or suitable to clothing industry? I shall indicate mailings, telephones and personal interview marketing communication tools to reflect the useful function to clothing industry.

Nowadays, clothing fashion products total change of market had changed rapidly and its new trends which has changed too rapidly suddenly after 1950 year. So, the different brands of clothing products need to be designed unique to satisfy clothing buyer individual specific groups and / or lifestyle needs. Also, the different design of fashion clothing products can represent every different clothing brand's image. However, sufficient promotion will be one influential tool to help the clothing product designer to promote is any kinds of cloths to let potential cloth clients to know or help it to build familiar brand image in the clothing market.

Good fashion design can challenge conventional views. It should be recognized their consumers very in the conservation they have towards fashion styles and also speed and readiness with which change their opinions. So, an efficient marketing communication strategy will let the clothing products designer to gather whose cloth clients' opinions in order to predict how they ought to decide to design preferable fashion styles choices more easily in order to let it follow general clothing product buyers' fashion styles design choice to design many attractive fashion styles of clothing products to let them to persuade them to choose to buy its clothing products more easily.

So, clothing buyer personal interviews or telephone individual contact or posting mail questionnaire enquiry promotion method will be one suitable to be used to promote in clothing industry. Because these market communication tools can gather any clothing buyer individual opinions in order to help the designers to understand. Then, clothing market can enhance the clothing design creating process and marketing personnel appreciate that within the fashion industry design can lead as well as respond to customer requirements progress can be made more easily. Thus, telephone, clothing buyers individual interview or questionnaire researching or post mailing questionnaire researching marketing communication tools will have effort to help the brand of clothing designer to predict how to design its cloths styles which can persuade potential clothing buyers to choose to buy its brands of any kinds of styles clothing products to wear more easily in possible. So, any clothing designer needs have a fashion marketing concept and have demonstrated equal concern for design, customers and profits. Thus, any clothing designer's marketing communication strategy needs to concentrate on fashion design promotion. It means that when the clothing product provider has good different styles of clothing design products and the suitable place( clothing stores) and the reasonable price setting , then it needs have good promotion ( communication tool) e.g. telephone, TV, radio, magazine etc. to its target audience ( e.g. child, young , old age , expensive or cheap clothing product buyer group, traditional design or popular fashion design style clothing product preference cloth buyers.

Nowadays, clothing communication medias include broadcast

advertisement ( TV and radio), print advertisement ( magazines and newspapers), brochures and booklets, posters and packaging, motion pictures, directories, display signs and symbols and logos. Any one of these communication medias can help any clothing designers to build its brand to be familiar to let its potential buyers to know. Instead of these communication media, sales promotion is usually connect closely with in clothing industry. The basic types of sales promotion include coupons, sampling , refunds and rebates, premiums and gifts , games, contexts. Any of these sale promotion will be one good communication method to persuade the clothing buyers to choose to attempt to buy the brand of any styles of clothing products to wear more easily. The primary communication objectives of these tools usually are: stimulation of clothing consume trials, increase of rebuy rates and reward of loyal customers in order to fasten he selling process. However, promotion should bot be used as an ongoing program, as it is only a short term taste. Otherwise, it can easily lower the price of the brand of clothing products.

The another kind communication tool is public relations, it means to build good relations with the clothing provider to public by obtaining favorable publicity. The " publics" are a the clothing provider's stakeholder, such as suppliers, employees, customers or governments, public relations activities can include press relationships, sponsorships, product placement, events management and crisis management. So, good public relation can help the clothing provider to build good brand image to let clothing buyers to know or familiar.

The final communication media is personal selling. It involves face-to-face activities, the clothing provider's clothing sales representatives of a particular clothing brand with the aim to inform, persuade or remind a clothing buyer to take appropriate action. The most common examples of personal selling include: sales presentations, sales meetings, incentive programs, samples, fairs and trade shows.

Consequently, any one of above communication medias will bring benefits to the clothing provider. However, the clothing provider needs to spend time and human resource and promotion communication tools resource to implement one effective marketing communication stragtegy to help its hw to promote its clothing products to let its potential clients to be familiar its different kinds of styles cloths more attractively. So, it seems on efficient communiation strategy can help the clothing provider to raise its different kinds of clothing design to attract its clothing buyers' consideration more easily.

# SIX

## Main Barriers Influence Artificial Intelligence Consumer Behavioral Prediction

In future, it is possible that these barriers will influence how to apply (AI technology) to predict consumer behavior in success. The barriers may include: Lacking of a (AI) digital data gathering vision and strategy, lacking of efficient workforce readiness, (AI) technology constraints., non reaching (AI) consumer behavioral prediction mature stage, time and money and resource constraints, law and regulations prohibition to develop (AI) consumer behavioral prediction bug data gather technology.

However, the recommendation of solutions to attack the barriers to influence artificial intelligence consumer behavioral prediction not success, it may include gaining employee buy in to participate and develop (AI) consumer behavioral prediction technology, making customer experience to a concern (AI) big data gather questionnaire investigation, providing compensation, training to employees in order to achieve (AI) consumer behavioral big data questionnaire investigation research digital technological goals and strategy, task senior leaders manage any (AI) digital big data gather technology changes, putting policies and (AI) big data gather digital technology in place to support a fully remote, flexible workforce in any (AI) digital big data gather questionnaires research projects, teaching all employees how to code/understand (AI) big data gather consumer behavioral prediction software development, appointing a chief (AI) officer to manage any (AI) big data gather customer behavioral prediction projects and automate everything and encourage customers to attempt experience to self-service and (AI) big data gather questionnaire research to earn beneficial consumption aim after they gave feedback to any (AI) digital questionnaire researches. So, in the future, the (AI) digital big data questionnaire researches can include these industries surveyed, such as automat m financial services, public healthcare, private healthcare, technology, telecoms, insurance, life sciences, manufacturing, media and entertainment, oil and gas, retail and consumer products etc.

Hence, in the future, any of these industries can attempt to apply (AI) digital big data gather technology to predict how and why consumer behaviors will change in order to avoid reducing consumer number threat occurrence.

5.1 (AI) digital data gather technology predicts food consumer behavior's main barriers

What are the main barriers to food industry? When the food manufacturer applies (AI) big data gather technology to predict food consumer behavior? The barriers include that the food manufacturer / provider needs to decide whether when the right time is applied to the right (AI) digital big data prediction tool channel to find the right food consumers to be chose to full food consumption satisfactory questionnaires, how to gather multi-class food consumption classifiers on real-world food consumers transactional data from the food sale domain consistently to show the critical numbers of different kinds of food items at which the predictive performance most accurate? So, any food manufacturer / provider's advanced in (AI) digital data gather warehousing and management technologies can provide that opportunities for food business to enhance long term relationship with the food providers' clients.

However, food industry's (AI) digital data gather aims to improve food customer product targeting, increase food customer loyalty and food purchase probability to the food supplier. To effective identify, understand and satisfy the needs of their food customers, the food suppliers need to develop the right (AI) digital questionnaire questions and find the right food customers to fill every right questions from every digital questionnaire at the right time through the right channel.

Above of all these, they will be the barriers when one food supplier expects its (AI) digital data gather questionnaires which can conclude the most accurate prediction concerns any kinds of consumer food product choices. So, such as (AI) digital data prediction model, it is needed to incorporate into the food market segmentation, food customer targeting, and food challenging decisions with the goal of maximizing the total food customer lifetime. For example, (AI) big data gather transaction data is reasonable and accurate for building predictive models. Transaction data can be electronically collected and readily made available for data mining in lot quantity at minimum extra costs.

Suggestion to apply (AI) prototypes of food customer profiles method to predict food customer behavioral changes. Prototypes of food customer profiles mean to be extracted from the discovered bins and multi-class classifies models are built using those prototypes. The learned models can than be used to predict the class of food customer profiles ( e.g. restaurants, school canteens, supermarkets etc. food suppliers) based on their food purchases. The approach is validated on the case study of a food retail and food service company operating in food and beverages market.

So, a food customer profile, it is a description (AI) data gather tool will record every of food customer using available information, which help in understanding their background and food consumption behavior. (AI) data gather tool can well develop every food customer profile, every food customer data is essential in food market analysis as they aid food suppliers in saving time and money by highlighting the real potential food consumers whose needs are to be met rather a range of individuals.

So, (AI) data gather tool can record every food consumer profile and every can be factual or behavioral food consumption. A factual food customer profile consists of a set of characteristics for (AI) big data gather record, e.g. demographic information , such as food customer name, gender, birth date, when a behavioral food customer profile consists of what the food customer is actually doing and is usually derived from (AI) digital transactional data gather record.

So, (AI) big data gather record's every behavioral food consumer profile can be much stronger predictor of the future food supplier consumption choice actions of a food customer. Furthermore, the food supplier's (AI) all past food consumer information that make up demographically based all past food customer profiles are expensive to acquire when the information for the food suppliers' past every food consumer food consumption behaviors. Moreover, food customer profile can be recorded to make real food purchase every time. So, when the food supplier finds the past food consumer's record from (AI) big data gather tool. Then, it can make more accurate judgement whether past every food consumer has chose to buy its food to eat how many times every year in order to predict whether its every past food consumer will choose to buy its foods how many times next year in possible. If the next year, its every past food consumer's consumption time to the food supplier is less than its current year consumption time. Then, the food supplier can attempt to find whether what factors to cause the past food consumers do not choose to increase food purchase times to the food supplier in current year. The factors may be possible be the food supplier's food prices are raised, food quality or taste is poor, the different kinds of food supply is shortage challenge, the food supplier's consumers lose confidence to buy the food supplier's foods to eat, when (AI) big data gather tool can help the food suppliers to find what the main factors to cause the past food consumer number to be reduced in order to predict how future food consumers' behavioral changes will be influenced from the food supplier's competitors in the global food supply market. Hence, (AI) big data gather tool can help every food supplier to attempt to find what the main factors to case the food supplier's food consumer number to be reduced as well as it can help the food supplier to predict how the food supplier's potential ( past not every purchase its any food consumers) food consumers who can be persuaded to choose to buy its foods to eat by learning what the main factors influence.

In conclusion, (AI) big data gather tool can help the food supplier to find what the main factors influence its past food consumers do not choose to buy its food more times or find what the main factors will attract its potential ( not ever buying its foods consumes) food consumers to choose to buy the food supplier's foods to eat.

5.2 The challenges of (AI) big data gather shaping
the future of retail for consumer industries

Another challenge of (AI) big data gather is that how to shape the consumer behavior to let business owner to feel or know or predict. It means that how it express it's conclusion or opinion for every consumer behavior after it had gather all big data in any data gather period, e.g. three months, half year or one year consumer shopping model data gather period.

Because every kind of industry, consumers will continue to demand price and quality change , with a wide range of convenient fulfilment options among of different kinds of products or services supply. Overall, the (AI) big data gather procedure gives opinion concerns every time retail experience will become more exciting, simple and convenient, depending on the consumer's ever-changing needs. So, I believe that (AI) big data gather every conclusion or result will be different, due to consumer's price and quality demand will often change to every kind of product or service supply in retail industry. So, how to shape (AI) big data gathering's analytical conclusion or result more clear. I shall recommend organizations need to build great understanding of and a stronger connection to increasingly empowered consumers before they plan and implement how to apply (AI) big data gather tool to predict consumer behavior as below:

Firstly, (AI) is empowered by technology, the consumer is redefining value. The traditional measures of cost, choice and convenience are still relevant, but not control and experience are also important. Globally, consumers have access to more than 2 billion different products choice by a wide range of traditional competitors and dynamic new entrants, all experimenting with new business models and methods of client engagement.

As choice increases, loyalty becomes more difficult familiarity and the consumer becomes more empowered. Businesses will have no choice and constantly innovate and disrupt themselves by meeting new technologies of high standards and expectations of consumers. So, (AI) data gather tool will need to follow different target group of consumers' needs to follow their different kinds of product design or style choice preferable to gather data in order to conclude the different target groups of consumer behavior to give opinion more clear and accurate to let businessmen to understand more clear how its customers' behavioral choice trend in the future half month, even to two years period.

Secondly, businessmen need to adopt changing technologies rapidly. Technology will be the key driver of this retail industry. Industry participants will only success if they have a clear prediction to focus on how to using technology to increase the value added to consumers. They must , however, do so will I realistic assessment of their costs and benefits. Hence, (AI) big data gather technological tools will need to design to help them to gather data efficiently by these ways, such as the internet of things ( IOT), artificial intelligence (AI) machine learning, augmented reality (AR)/virtual reality (VR), digital traceability. So, future (AI) big data gather tool are predicted to be most influential customer behavioral positive emotion changing tool for retail , due to their widespread applications , ability to drive efficiencies and impact on labor in order to impact consumer behavior changing effort from negative emotion to positive.

Thirdly, (AI) big data gather tool is an advanced data science of consumer behavior predictive tool. Businesses will have to bring the journey from simply collecting consumer data to using it to scale and systematize enhanced decision making across the entire value chain. When focused on their business goals, industry players should not lose sight of the impact that future capabilities and transformative business models may have on society.

However, (AI) big data gather tool will encounter these challenges when any business plans and implements to apply it to predict consumer behavior in retail industry. The challenges include that as below:

1. The high cost and difficulty of implementing new technologies . The (AI) big data gather tool needs capital and capabilities to be designed to implement to be applied to different retail industry users. so, expensive barriers to innovation, an organization and the skillsets of its people to support a new design of (AI) big data gather tool, highly digital technology may be required.

2. Slow pace of cultural change. Consumers need to adapt or accept (AI) new technology consumption model in the traditional retail industry. The rate of change is outpacing the ability of businesses to keep up. (AI) big data gather tool needs to be designed to adopt in new or evolved business model requires, in most cases, a new level of customer behavioral predictive machine operation will impact to influence any retail businesses' consumer behavioral changes at a minimum, an organization's structure, capabilities, culture and decision making. If the retail business expects to apply (AI) big data gather tool to predict how to change its consumer behaviors and how their consumption behaviors will tend to change in order to achieve to change their positive emotion from negative emotion before they choose to buy its product or consume its service in success.

5.3 Challenge to using (AI) neural networks to predict customer behavior from big data gather tool

(AI) big data gather tool will encounter the challenge: How can predict customer behavior be represented as sequential data describing the interactions of the customer with a company or an (AI) data gather system through the time, e.g. these interactions are items that the customer purchase or views ? So, every customer data gather , (AI) needs to spend time to analyze how and why to cause whose consumption behavioral choice. It is too difficult matter or judgement for (AI) learning. So, (AI) needs to spend time to learn how to analyze every customer's shopping behavior or actin in order to gather all different consumers' past shopping action information in order to help business owners to predict future its potential customer shopping behavior how to change more clear and accurate prediction.

(AI) big data gather tool needs to learn to know that how to judge every customer interaction likes purchases over time can be represented with sequential data. Sequential data has the main property that the order of the information is important. Many (AI) machine learning models are not suited for sequential data, as they consider each input sample independent from previous ones. Therefore, at the end of the sequence, (AI) big data gather learn machines need to keep in their internal state of every customer purchase data, kind of product or service, price , whole year consumption times form all previous inputs, making them suitable for this type of data.

However, consumer behavior can be represented as sequential data describing the interactions through the time. Examples of these interactions are the items that the user purchases or views. Therefore, the history of interactions can be modeled as sequential data, which has the particular trial that an incorporate a temporal aspect. For example, if a user buys a new mobile phone, who might purchase accessories for this mobile phone in the near future or it the user buys a electronic book or paper book , he might be interested in books by the same author. Therefore, to make accurate predictions is important to model this temporal aspect correctly. To solve this predictive challenge of consumers to buy the product. One count the number of purchased products of a particular category in the last N days, or the number of days since the last purchase.

So, the (AI) big data gather designers can attempt to produce a feature vector which can be fed into a machine learning algorithm such as " logistic regression" will be the main feature and function to any (AI) big data gather machine to learn how to apply this " logistic regression" function or feature to predict any customer behavioral change for any product purchase or service consumption to the (AI) predictive consumer behavioral business users. Every different kinds of product purchases or services consumption will be needed to design " different model of logistic regression" in order to follow the kind of business to predict whose consumer purchase or service consumption behavior to predict more accurate.

5.4 Challenges of artificial intelligence, algorithms technology and machine learning impact to consumption market

Markets have played a key role in providing individuals and businesses with the opportunity to gain from trade. If (AI) big data gather tool can predict how to change potential customer behavior in success. The challenges to consumers will face that the overall market consumption model will be dominated by the businessmen only. So, it is not fair or reasonable to consumers, because (AI) big data gather tool has controlled or dominated all consumers' minds and it has predicted how and why every kind of product or service consumer shopping model or consumption behaviors how will change.

It will bring this questions: How can market designers learn the characteristics necessary to set optimal, or at least better, reserve prices after they had gather all data to conclude the analytical results of their consumers behaviors how will change? How can market designers better learn the environments of their markets?

In response to these challenges, artificial intelligence (AI ) and machine learning are important tools for market design. For example, retailers and marketplaces , such as eBay, Amazon and many others are mining their vast amounts of data to identity patterns that help them create better shopping experiences for their clients and increase the efficiency of their markets. By having better prediction tools, these and their companies can predict and better manage dynamic consumption market environments. The improved forecasting that (AI) and machine learning algorithms provide help marketplaces and retailers better anticipate consumer demand and producer supply as well as help target products and activities for segmented markets. Another important application of (AI) 's strength in improving forecasting to help markets operate more efficiently is in electricity market example. To operate efficiently, electricity marker makers can attempt to apply (AI) machine learning tool to follow every household family electricity consumers' past electricity consumption record to judge ( predict) how it will be every family's forecasting in the year.

An inaccurate forecast in the electricity supply and demand that can dramatically affect electricity market bad supply outcomes causing high variance in electricity charge prices or worse, blackouts. By better predicting every family's electricity demand and supply , electricity market makers can better allocate power generation to the most efficient power sources and maintain a more reasonable electricity stable charge market. Any example is design market, the application of (AI) algorithms to market design are already widespread and diverse.

(AI) algorithms technology , it is a safe that (AI) will play a growing role in the design and implementation of market over a wide range of applications. The challenges are that how (AI) can guarantee accurate to predict when and why and how consumer behavioral changes to any retail industries. In fact, retailers will need to discover the value that (AI) can bring to what benefits to influence their customer behaviors.

In the future, (AI) will bring their benefits to influence customers to build positive emotions to any retailers in these aspects as below:

1. Future (AI) big data gather tool will be an area of compute science that deals with giving machines , the ability to seem like they have human intelligence. In short, it is the power of a machine to copy intelligent human behavior. For example, machine learning algorithms are being integrated into analytics and customer relationship management platforms to uncover information on how to better serve customers, chat bots have been incorporated into websites to provide immediate service to customers.

2. (AI) adoption continue to rise with chat bots taking the lead. Due to increasing ease of deployment , instant availability and improved quality, chat bots will become more and more common to manage customer service queries and to make intelligent purchase recommendations. Also, retailers can engage this kind of technology to answer continue questions and supplement customer support with chat-based shopping experience. So, (AI) and declines personalized, customized and localized experiences to customers.

(AI) will be applied across the entire retail product and service cycle, firm manufacturing to post-sale customer service interactions. Hence, retailers can use (AI) to its fullest potential will be also to influence purchases in the moment and anticipate future purchases, guiding shoppers towards the right products in a regular and highly personalized manner.

3. (AI) technology can rise the conscious customers. Customers are demanding an increased interest in the ethical practice of the brands they buy from. Todays, customers have a well-developed sense of what is solely intended to drive sales. This has lead to a rise in consumers ho make values based judgements about what to buy and where to shop. These consumers believe their purchase habits have an impact on the world. To win customers, retailers need have good conscious to predict consumers' desire. Future, (AI) data gather technology will be a good consumer behavior predictive tool to predict about for years will now become customer expectations and will have drastically changed the path to purchase. So, (AI) data gather tool is the predictive consumer expectations tool on every interaction, they have these brands.

4. Future (AI) can be impacted to influence consumer behaviors by its potential to free up time, enhance, quality, and enhance personalization. The industries include: Healthcare industry can apply (AI) to support diagnosis by detecting variations in patient data, early identification of potential pandemics, imaging diagnostics; automat industry can apply (AI) to autonomous fleets to ride sharing, semi-autonomous features, such as driver assist, engine monitoring and predictive, autonomous maintenance; financial service industry can apply (AI) to design the suitable personalized financial planning, fraud detection and anti-money laundering and automation of customer operation; transportation and logistics industry can apply (AI) to autonomous trucking and delivery, traffic control and reduced congestion and enhanced security; technology, media and telecommunications industry can apply (AI) to search media, and recommendation, customized content creation and personalized marketing and advertising to attract retailers to promote; retail and consumer industry can apply (AI) to design personalized production, anticipating customer demand, , inventory and delivery management; energy industry can apply (AI) to read and record smart metering , more efficient grid operation and storage and predictive maintenance; manufacturing industry can apply (AI) to enhance monitoring and auto-correction of processes, supply chain and production optimization and on-demand production.

Hence, future (AI) technology will impact consumer technology when any retailers apply it to assist its manufacturing processes or product sale or service provision processes to satisfy consumers' needs, it means that it can help any retailers to influence positive emotion to consumers in their whole sale or consumption or purchase processes

5. (AI) and machine learning technologies make it possible to capture, process, and inter data on a massive scale effectively , then any human being could ever do. For example, Criteo's creative technology " Kinetic design" can apply insights from 1.2 billion monthly impressions to select and optimize individual branded advertisements components according to each shopper's preference and intent. This ensures more personalization and visually inspiring on brand ads. resulting in up to 12% more sales for (AI) technology advertiser clients.

Moreover, advertisers can now engage and inspire shoppers on a more personal level, rendering custom ads. it real-time for every impression. So, designer continues to learn from each design's success to make ads. more and more effective over time. Furthermore, brands are increasingly using paid search on retail sites to draw attention to their products on the crowded online shelf, e.g. Google shopping is a key growth area's more users are engaging with shopping ads. and across the globe. Google shopping has become essential to retailers' marketing strategies, but is a difficult channel to apply its tool to be promoted effectively . Thus, future (AI) and machine -learning technologies can dramatically improve digital commerce performance application to apply (AI) and machine learning to digital consumer. So, future (AI) technology can be applied to digital commerce aspect, it will fall into the categories of pattern recognition, classification, prediction and consumer behavior.

In conclusion, the benefits of using (AI) in digital commerce include: improved efficiency in discovering the relationships between datasets over traditional methods, which require complex modeling and coding, improved accuracy for clearly defined processes that involve a lot of manual processing, ability to deal with a large emotion of data with many attributes, for example: customer behavior data, multichannel and multi-device data , complex product data and fraud detection, more accurate analysis, such as customer segmentation sentiment, analysis and personalization frequent algorithum refreshes, such as several times a day, to capture the changes in customer and market behavior.

Finally, however, a lot of types predictive consumption behavior around (AI), in particulars that driven by vendors claiming their solutions are (AI) , ready and can deliver dramatic improvements over existing technologies. Application leaders for digital commerce can be misled into believing that

(AI) can solve all their problems, which is not true for n in-depth discussion of the (AI) consumers and market behavioral predictive tool and machine -learning technologies bot. Thus, (AI) prediction consumer behavioral technology can give beneficial quantitative analysis for forecasting in business and market especially in consumer behavior and in the consumer decision-making process ( consumer choice model) more effectively and efficiently.

Is Artificial Intelligent the most effective and accurate consumer behavioral tool?

Is (AI) the best and the most effective and accurate consumer behavioral prediction tool to compare other kinds of consumer behavioral prediction tools? Nowadays, retailing competitions are serious businessmen often find different kinds of methods to attempt to predict consumer changes. The consumer behavioral predictive methods can include as these below methods, instead of (AI) big data gathering tool.

Firstly, statistics is the popular mathematic method, it applies auto-regression, liner regression, structural equation modelling, logistic regression statistic techniques to be used to predict consumer behaviors. Secondly, it is classification method, it sis a support vector machine to assist businessmen to make consumer behavioral prediction, it also includes decision making tress diagram technique. Thirdly, it is rule mining method, it is algorithm, market base analytic etc. business marketing concept analytical tool, it also includes graph mining technique tool. Next, it is psychological prediction model tool, it is psychology prediction model too, it is a kind of psychological method to predict consumer behaviors. Finally, it is the most updated and potential artificial neural network (ANN) machine tool, it gathered big data, then it will carry on analyzing and applies psychological method to conclude the most accurate and reasonable solutions to give recommendation to businesses to predict when and how and why their consumer behaviors will change. So, it is one owned human mind's machine and owned psychological and analytical efforts to replace humans to make any judgement in order to make the most accurate predictive behavioral changes for consumers, instead of the traditional marketing concept and psychological and mathematic methods to predict consumer behavior, (AI) big data gathering tool will be another new tool.

What are the advantages of (AI) tool to be used to predict consumer behaviors as well as what are the different between it and other traditional consumer behavioral predictive tools? I shall explain as below:

Firstly, as above all case studies are explained to (AI) questionnaire design method benefit, I believe (AI) big data gathering tool can be applied to help human to analyze and design any the suitable valid questions to enquire any kinds of business consumers in order to gather the most meaning and useful opinions to conclude the most accurate consumer behavioral prediction for every questionnaire. So, future (AI)'s analytical effort and decision making effort most be exceed above human's judgement efforts. So, future (AI) can help human to design the most useful and meaning different kinds of valid questionnaire ( survey) questions as well as assist humans to analyze and make accurate decision making and conclusions to give opinions to help businessmen to predict when consumer behaviors will change and how their consumption behaviors will change to influence their businesses in order to help them to make any efficient and effective and accurate solutions to avoid consumer number to be decreased and the most important benefit is that it can give opinions to help businessmen to explain why ( what the factors ) cause their consumer behaviors change suddenly. It will be human's efforts can not achieve to exceed (AI)'s efforts in the future.

Secondly, (AI) can make artificial machine judgement and analytical effort, without human misleading or unfair or unreasonable judgement. So, it can make more fair and reasonable and accurate conclusion to give opinions to predict when, how and why consumer behaviors will change suddenly to the kind of business in customer model building process and evaluating the results of customer relationship management –related investment more accurate.

Furthermore, (AI) big data gathering tool will help businesses to improve the success rate of acquiring customers, increasing sales and establishing competitiveness. (AI) big data gathering tool can give opinions how to build customer loyalty to be positive emotion impact and it can find solutions to avoid every client's negative emotion causes to bring complaints behavior to the businessman's product or service. For example, Telecom industry and aggressive research has been conducted in this by applying various data mining techniques to avoid long distance phone call users' complaints. If gathered any long distance phone call users' past complaint data to record what are their general complaint issues. Then, (AI) tool will analyze all these past complaint issues to conclude and give opinions to let Telecom knows whether which aspects encounter challenge that Telecom needs to improve it's long distance phone call services or functions in order to satisfy

Telecom's long distance phone call users' needs for long term. After Telecom attempted to improve its services and/ or functions from (AI) opinions and solution methods, when it fell it's long distance phone call users have positive emotions to satisfy its service performance and function performance. Then, it can prove (AI) tool's opinions and solutions are useful. The consequence is that their complain numbers will be decreased and they won't plan to choose another long distance phone call telephone service company to replace Telecom long distance phone call service more easily.

So, (AI) big data gathering tool can concentrate on finding focus on components of customer relationship management method and datasets more accurate and efficient and effective than human's data gathering and analytical effort. It implies (AI) big data gathering tool has unique more efficient and effective and accurate dataset gathering and analytical and judgement and decision making effort, it is human can not achieve.

Thirdly, (AI) big data gathering tool has much customer loyalty predictive effort. It's effort is more easily subsequently selected, reviewed and classified to compare human's gathering data effort in whole data gathering and analytical process.

In (AI) big data gathering process, (AI) can organize whole big data gathering process and technique more easily in short time. It will include these four steps. The first stage is that customer identification stage, customer identification also known as acquisition has to do with targeting the population , who are most likely to become customer segmentation. So, (AI) can help different kinds of businesses to gather their competitors' consumer purchase behavior data in short time, it is human can not achieve. The second stage is that customer attraction stage, after (AI) maker has been segmented for the business when it has ensured to gather the businessman's global competitors' consumers data. Then it analyze these all data to find solutions / methods to give the best opinions to the organizations how to achieve the direct effort and resources into attracting the target customer segments. The third stage is that customer retention, it can be defined as the activity that an organization undertakes in order to reduce customer defections. TO be successful, customer retention starts with the first contact on organization has with a customer and continues throughout the entire lifetime of a relationship involves loyalty programs, one to one marketing and complaints management. SO, (AI) can consist the business to find the best or the most reasonable , efficient , effective solutions or methods and it will conclude all these solutions to find the most reasonable and useful opinions to achieve to the aim to help the business to reduce customer complain numbers and help the business to build confident loyalty relationship between it and its clients. SO, (AI)'s analytical effort and decision making effort can be more accurate than human's analytical effort and decision making effort. IT can achieve it's consumer behavioral predictive aim more accurate and efficient and effective in the shortest time to compare human.

Fourthly, (AI) big data gathering tool can design more accurate dataset program for questionnaire (survey) to compare human's questionnaire ( survey ) effort. It means that (AI) can spend less time to research and make judgement what are the most reasonable and meaning questions for different kinds of businesses' needs. This includes data conduction a questionnaire, survey or interview of the individual or environment researched, public data repository: This includes commercially available public data; organizational data; this contains data collected from an organizational database, organizational information system. For example, their website log details etc. It also includes company transactional data, data purchased from a company.

For example, one vehicle sale company expects to research all global vehicle sale companies' past the different kinds of vehicle styles, design sale number data, the different kinds of vehicle style, design sale price data, every country's vehicle consumer number to the vehicle purchase number data to the vehicle company in short time. (AI) big data gathering tool can help the vehicle sale company to gather all any one for these global vehicle sale competitors' past data in the short time. It is human effort, who can not achieve this efficient, effective and accurate data gathering aim for this vehicle sale company. Even, when (AI) had gathered all global it's vehicle competitors' past sale data, (AI) can make more accurate analytical and judgement and decision making effort to design different kinds of questionnaire ( survey) questions to prepare to enquire it's different target segmentation vehicle potential clients in order to predict what are their needs to choose to buy any vehicles from the vehicle company. SO, (AI) tool can conclude more accurate conclusions and give the most reasonable and useful opinions to let the vehicle company to know in order to predict what are it's potential vehicle buyer's needs and manufacture the suitable vehicle styles or designs to raise their vehicle purchase desires.

Fifthly, (AI) tool is only one perfect tool for big data gathering in order to achieve accurate results and increased profit. What is (AI) big data gathering mean? The term " big data" gathering describes the accumulation and analytical of vast amounts of information, but big data is much more than a big amount of data. It is also the ability to extract meaning to sort through big volumes of numbers and find the hidden patterns, unexpected correlations and surprising connections that can be used in different industries like medical field, security and protection field or marketing that adopt " big data driven" decision making enjoy significantly greater productivity than those that do not. So, the benefits of (AI) is given to the company by using big data repaid complexity of implementation projects and hence project risks, when accelerating time to value. It is why that human's gathering effort can not replace ( A I ) data gathering effort.

All analysing above benefits to (AI) big data benefits to any organizations, it brief this question: How can (AI)apply big data gathering and analysing to predict when and how any why consumer behavior will change suddenly? The purchase decision making process is consumers reducing purchase choice behaviors.

Consumers are being considered pure rational beings ( consumer tried only to satisfy self-interest). Hence, due to future (AI) owns human's psychological , analytical , emotional predictive, purchasing decision making effort.

( A I ) will be assumed to sees one customer how who will make purchase decisions. So, after the (AI) gathered all data concerns the find of business's past customer segmentation purchase activities, e.g. age, sex,. Income level, the product's style sale number, the product price variable sale etc. different kinds complex data.

It can make more accurate psychological and analytical effort to predict when the business's consumer behaviors will change as behaviors will change as well as find what reasons their consumption behaviors will change and how trend of their consumer behaviors will change more accurate. For example, today there are a lot of industries that use big data: healthcare (treatment ) becoming personalized and patient centric and predictive analysis are used to prevent diseases for example Angelina Jolie under event a predictive double mastectomy after learning she had 87% rich to developing breast cancer, sports ( by using sensors data are collected from players during a game in order to improve their playing schemes), weather(more than 60 years of global weather analysis are used to predict the risk of future extreme events), logistics ( smart tucks and smart species, agriculture (monitoring weather and soil conditions for optimum point of harvesting).

Consequently, due to the evolving consumer demands, and the ever growing digitization, the world is digitally transforming which means the new technologies are needed to be used and driven significant business improvement. So, such as why (AI) tool will be our future main predictive tool to help businesses to predict when, how and why their potential customer behavioral will change. Big data is one of the our channels through digital transformation is made, together with cloud, mobile and networks. The challenges for digital transforming and therefore using A I big data gathering tool as main technology are: digital proficiency, legacy systems, security and jobs becoming absolute.

In the future, big data can use data from text to picture , sounds, movies, music satellite coordinates or any other type of input or output data that type of input or output data that came from different influential aspect. It is cloud solutions, bring big data will be for predict insight driven by business strategy, new product strategies and new consumer relationship, predictive consumer behavioral strategy. Using the right data in the right business decision will mean smart decisions, new opportunities and utimately a big competitive advantage. Hence (AI) big data gathering tool is different is that (AI) can be one depth in-memory database function, it can make real-time data analytics that provide meaningful information in short time, it is also the visualization tool , such as SAP Lumira, allow this exploration and understanding of the data, and ultimately supports the decision making process. All above these features, which will be human's data gathering effort who won't exceed (AI) big data gathering effort. Hence, future (AI)big data gathering will be the best choice to assist businesses to predict consumer behaviors successfully.

Reference

Adrian, P. (2012). Introduction to marketing theory & practice, 3 rd edition, London: Oxford press.

Ajzen, I (1991). The theory of planned behavior. Organizational behavior and human decision processes, 50(2), 179-211. doi: 10.1016/0749.5978 (91) 90020-7.

Alba, Joseph W. and J. Wesley Hutchinson (1987). " Dimensions Of Consumer Expertise", Journal of consumer research, 13 March, 411-454.

Bailey, L., Mokhtarian, P.L. Little, A. (2008). The broader Connection Between Public Transportation, Energy Conservation And Greenhouse Gas Reduction, Report Prepared As Part Of TCRP Project J-11/Tasks Transit Cooperative Research Program, Transportation Research Board Submitted To American Public Transportation Association in http://www.apta.com/research/into/online/land_use.cfmi, accessed 17 April 2008.

Baucer, R,"Consumer Bhavior As Risk Taking , In Risk Taking And Information handling In Consumer Behavior", D. Coxceds Harvard University Press, Cambridge, Mass 1976.

Biederman, P. (2008). Travel and tourism, Pearson Prentice Hall, New Jersey.

Bogers, R. P., Brug, J. Van Assema, P., & Dagnetie, P.C. (2004) , Explaining fruit and vegetable consumption: The theory of planned behavior and misconception of personal intake level. Appetite, 42,157-166.

Bolton, Ruth N. (1998), " A Dynamic Model Of The Duration Of The Customer's Relationship With A Continuous Service Provider: The Role Of Satisfaction", Marketing Science, 17 (1), 45-65.

B.Shiv and A. Fedorikhin, " Heart And Min In Conflict: The Interplay Of affect And Cognition In Consumer Decision Making", J. Consumer Res., vol. 26, pp. 278-292, Dec. 1999.

Brown, K.W., Ryan, R.M. Reswell , J.D. (2007). Mindfulness: Theoretical Foundatins And Evidence For Its Salutary Effects. Psychological Inquiry, 18, 211-237.

Burke, R.R. : Behavioral effects of digital signage, J. Advertising Res. 49(2), 180-185 (2009).

Cant, M., Brink , A. & Brijall, S., Consumer behavior, Cape Town, South Africa: Juta, 2006.

Conner, M. & Abraham, C. (2001). Conscientiousness and the theory of planned behavior: Toward a more complete model of the antecedents of intention and behavior. Social psychology bulletin, 27, 1547-1561.

Cooper C. Mallon, K, Leadbetter S, Pollack L, Peipins ( 2005) , cancer internet search activity on a major search engine, United States 2001 to 2003, J Med Internet Res. 7(3): e36.

Cope, R. R. Cope and H. Davis (2008). Disney's virtual Queues: A strategic opportunity to co-brand services ? Journal of Business & economics research, vol. 6 no10, 13-20.

Cornelia, B.F. (1999) Rural development news, the North Central Regional Center For Rural Development vol. no 24 , IOWA.

Couper, M.P. J. Blair and T. Triplet ( 1999). A Comparison Of Mail And E-mail For a Survey Of Employees In USA Statistical Agencies. Journal Of Official Statistics, 15, 39-56.

David J. Nowak & Gordon M. Melsler (2016) " Air quality effects of urban trees and parks." National recreation and park association, USA.

Data monitor ( 2008). The proctor and gamble company. Retrieved Nov. 15 2009 from http://www.datamonitor.com/

De Hollander, A. E. M., J.M. Melse, Elebret & P. G.N. Kramers ( 1999), " An Aggregate public health indicator to represent the impact of multiple environmental exposures" Epidemiology: 606-617.

De Visser, R.O., & McDonnell, E.J. ( 2013). " Man points": Masculine capital and young men's health. Health psychology, 32( 1), 5-14. doi:10. 1037/ a0029045.

Dunn, J & A Neumsister (2002). Knowledge management in the Information age. E. business review, Fall , 37-45. Jounral of service, spring 2011, vol. 4, no1, De Grovte (2009).

Dyer, D., F. Dalzell & R. Olegario ( 2004). Rising tide. Lessons learned from 165 years of brand building at Procter and Gamble. Boston, MA: Havard Business School Press.

Eysenbach G (2006) Infodemiology: Tracking flu- related searches on the web for syndromic surveillance. American Medical Informatics Associaion Annual Symposium Proceedings , Curran Associates, Red Hook, NY, pp. 244-248.

Ettredge M, Gerdes, J. Karuga , G (2005) Using web- based search data to predict macro-economic statistics. Commun ACM 48: 87-92.

Felce, D. and Perry, J. (1995). Quality of life: A contribution to its definition and measurement, vol. 16, no.1 pp: 51-74.

Feldman, Jack M. And John G. Lynch Jr. (1988), "Self-Generated Validity And Other Effects Of Measurement On Belife, Attitude, Intention And Behavior", Journal of applied psychology, 73(3),421-35.

Fiese, M, Hofmann, W., & Wanke, M (2009). The impulsive consumer. Predicting consumer behavior with implicit reaction time measurement. In M. Wanke (ed.) Social psychology of consumer behavior (pp.335-364). New York, NY: Psychology press.

Fitzsimons, Gavan, J. And Vicki G. Morwitz ( 1996), " The Effect Of Measuring Intent On Brand-Level
Purchase Behavior", Journal of consumer research, 23 (1), 1-11.

Hallerman , D. (2008) video Advertising Online: Spending And Pricing , New York. E-Marketer.

Harriet Griffey. (2010) The art of concentration, enhance focus, Reduce, stress and achieve move. Macmillan publishers ltd,Basinastoke and Oxford, London UK.

Helleman, D. (2008) Video Advertising Online: Spending And Pricing , New York, E-Marketer.

Hensen, C. (2003). Kreuzfahrtourismus.www.christoph- hensen.de/ Facharbeit.pdf.

Huang, H.I. (2012). An empirical analysis of the strategic Management of competitive advantage: a case study of higher technical and vocational education in Taiwan ( Doctoral dissertation,
Victoria University).

Jamieson, Linda F. And Frank M. Bass ( 1989), " Adjusting Stated Intention Measures To Predict Trial Purchase Of New Products: A Comparison Of Models And Methods," Journal of marketing research, 26 ( August), 336-45.


Korea Ministry Of Environment. Public Organizations spend 2.2 Trillon Korean Won To Purchase green Products in 2014; Ministry Of Environment: Sejoung, Korea, 2015.

Kremers, S.P. J., De Bruijn, G.J., droomers, M., Van Lenthe, F. J., & Brug, J. (2005). Environmental interventions for selected dietary behaviors in adults. In J. Brug & F. J. Van Lenthe ( eds.) , Environmental determinants and interventions for physical activity, nutrition and smoking: A review pp. 282-315. Rotterdam: Erasmus Medical Center.

Lee, D.; Kim, M. ; Lee, J. adoption of green electricity policies: Investigating the role of environmental attitudes via big data-driven search-queries. Energy policy 2016. 90, 187-201.

Lee, Terrence, " Tech in Asia-connecting Asia's startup system " Tech. in Asia-connecting Asia's startup ecosystem, N.p.,4 July 2016.

Los Angeles Country Department Of public Health (2016), Country Health Ranking Model, Retrieved From www.countryhealthrankgings.org/our-approach. USA.

Mayne, Lonnie. " Evolve of die in the age of the consumer". Entrepreneur, N.P. , 16 Apr. 2014. web of Oct. 2016.

McGregor, S.L. T., & Goldsmith, E.B. (1998). Expanding our understanding of quality of life, standard of living and well-being. Journal of family and consumer science, 90(2), 2-6, 22.

McMichael, A.J. M. Mckee, J. Shkolnikov and T. Valkanen ( 2004), " Morality trends and setbacks, global convergence or divergence?", Lancet 363, 1155-1159.

Melse, J.M. & A.E. M. De Hollander (2001). " Human Health And The Environment", background document for the OECD Environmental Outlook, OECD, Paris.

Moschis, George p. & Roy, L. Moore ( 1979), " Decision making among the young. A socialization perspective " Journal of consumer research , 6 ( September).

Mulligan, M. Banerjee, T & Thomas, N. (2008) ,European Paid Content And Activity Forecast, (2008 to 2013), Jupiter Research.

Peter, J., Ryan, M, M, " An Investigation Of Perceived Risk At The Brand Level, " Journal of marketing research, 13 May 1976, pp. 184-188.

Pieters, R., & Wedel, M. (2007). Goal Control Of Visual Attention To Advertising: The Yarbus Implication. Journal Of Consumer Research, 34, 224-233 ( August).

Parasuaman, and Leonard L. Berry (1985), " Problems And Strategies In Sevices Marketing", Journal of marketing, 49 ( Spring), 33-46.

Priesnitz, W. (2007) Counting Our Food Miles. Natural Life, 1 July.

R.C. Oliver, " When is consumer loyalty?" J.Marketing vol. 63, pp.33-44.1999.

Reggiani, A . (ed). 1998, accessibility, trade and locational behavior, Ashgate publishing ltd, England.

Rushe, D. (2013) " The 10 best paid CEO in America". The Guardian , 22 Oct, ( online). Available at:
http://www.theguardian.com/business/2013/Oct22/best-paid-chief-executives-america (Accessed: 3 May 2014).

Spiekermann and Wegener (2007), update of selected potential accessibility indicators. Final report, urban and regional research ( S&W), RRG spatial planning and geoinformation. ESPON. Available online
at http:// <www.espon.eu/mmp/online/website/ contentprojects/947/1297/ file_2724/espon_accessibility_update-2006-fr_070207.pdf>, accessed on 1 July 2009.

Starbucks (2014) Our company available at http:// www. starbucks.com/ about- us/company-information ( accessed: 3 May 2014).


Shostack, G. Lynn ( 1984), " Designing Services That Deliver", Harvard Business Review, 62 ( January-February), 133-9.

Shostack, G. Lynn (1985), " Planning The Service Encounter ,in the service encounter" , John A. Czepiel, Michael R. Solomon, and Carol F. Suprenant, eds. New York: Lexington Books, 243-54.

Shostack, G. Lynn (1987), " Service Positioning Through, Structural Change", Journal of marketing, 51 ( Janurary), 34-43.

Soloman, Michael R. (1985), "Packaging The Service Provider", Service Industries Journal , 5(1), 64-71.

Stevens, C.W. (1980), "K-MartStores Try New Look To Invite More Spending" The Wall Street Journal, Nov. 26, 29-35.

Sullivan, Nicholas P(2007). You can hear me now: How Micro loans and cell phones are connecting the world, San Francisco, CA: John Wilsey & Sans, 2007.


T. Ambler, A. Ioannides, And S. Rose, " Brand s On The Brain : Neuroimages Of Advertising ", Business Strategy rev., vol. 11, 3. pp. 17-30. 2000.

Westbrook, Robert A. ( 1980), " Intrapersonal affective influences on consumer satisfaction with products, " Journal of consumer research , 7 ( June) 49-54.

Wiig, k.(1993). Knowledge management foundations: Thinking About thinking. How people and organizations create, represent and use knowledge vol.1 , of knowledge management series schema press: Arlington, TX.

World Health Organization (2003). Diet, nutrition and the prevention of Chronic diseases report of a joint WHO/FAO. expert consultation. Geneva: World Health Organization.

Wysocki, B. (1979), " Sight, Smell, Sound: They're all arms in retailer's arsenal" The Wall Street Journal, Nov. 17, 1979. 1-35.

Yale Center For Environmental Law And Policy (2006). Environmental Performance Index. Data available on-line at http://epi.yale.edu

• 94 •

# SEVEN

# HUMAN BEHAVIOR HOW INFLUENCES (AI) -DRIVEN AUTOMATION INDUSTRY DEVELOPMENT

1.1 (AI) - driven automation industry development how to influence work nature change

On positive benefit hand, it is possible that (AI) -driven automation industry will create wealth and expand economy growth to any countries, but it will be accompanied by changed in the skills that workers need to learn, if the low skill workers expect to avoid unemployment threat when (AI) technology can replace their jobs in future one day. Thus, it is possible that (AI) technology will also bring negative influence to cause low skill worker unemployment challenge in the applied (AI) technology countries.

For the low skill worker unemployment reason, it is because that one of main ways that technology increases productivity is by decreasing the number of labor hours needed to create a unit of output. It implies (AI) technology will influence low educated and low skillful labor number to be decreased ( reduction employment number).

Will (AI) bring benefits to the employers? In contrast, technological change tended to work in a different direction throughout the nowadays. The advance of computer and the internet raised the relative productivity of higher skilled workers. So, routine-intensive occupations that focused on predictable tasks disappearance, such as switch board, operators, filming checkers, travel agents and assembling line workers etc. were particularly replaced by new technologies. However, today, it may be challenging to predict exactly which jobs will be most immediately affected by (AI) driven-automation. The reason is because (AI) is not a single technology, but rather a collection of technologies that are felt unevenly through the economy to influence job changing both negatively and positively.

In positively view point, (AI) driven-automation will make many workers more productive and increase demand for certain skills. Consequently, new jobs are likely to be directly create in areas , such as the development and supervision of (AI) as well as indirectly created in a range of areas throughout the economy as higher incomes lead to expanded demand. So, (AI) will bring macro economy advantages in possible.

Otherwise, in negatively view point, many traditional human needed ( demand) skillful jobs will be threatened by automation are highly concentrated among lower-paid, lower-skilled and less -educated workers. It means automation will cause pressure on demand for this group, pressure and employment, if (AI) can replace the low skilled and less educated workers' jobs. Thus, (AI) will have negative influence to impact on the labor market.

(AI) capabilities will enable automation of some tasks that have long required human labor. Can (AI) replace some simple human jobs? If (AI) can replace some simple human jobs, then it is possible to cause unemployment if employers applied (AI) machines to replace the low skill workers to do their simple jobs in future one day. For example, advances in robotics are expanding machines' abilities to interact with and sharp the physical world. Combined , (AI) and robotics will give rise to smarter machines that can perform more sophisticated functions than ever before and brings more advantages that humans have exercised. This will permit automation of many tasks now performed by human workers and could change the shape of the labor market and human activity. It depends on whether employers choose to reduce all worker numbers to be replaced by (AI) machines or employers choose to apply (AI) machines to assist the low skillful workers to work more efficient or raise performance and productivities. If future employers apply (AI) machines to assist workers to raise performance and efficiency, then the unemployment challenge won't cause, due to the number of worker won't reduce. But if employers decide to unemploy all low skillful workers and they are replaced by (AI) machines, then the unemployment challenge will cause in possible.

1.2 How (AI) influences labor market

Today, it may be challenging to predict exactly which jobs will be most immediately affected by (AI)-driven automation. Because (AI) is not a single technology, but rather a collection of technologies that are applied to specific tasks.

Some specific predictions are possible based on the current (AI) technology. For example, driving jobs and house cleaning jobs, bank counter service jobs, telephone enquiry service operators. Restaurant cooking jobs, simple accounting record service jobs etc. that require relatively less education to perform. Advancements in computer vision and related technologies have made the feasibility of fully appear more likely, potentially displacing some workers in driving-dominant professions. Seemingly similar robot, for which the operational tasks is less specific of navigating to a specific destination when following a set of given rules and preserving safety.

In the future, the effects of (AI) on the labor market in the decade ahead will continue the trend toward skill-biased change that computerization and communication innovations have driven in recent decades. Thus, some human driving occupation will be disappeared or replaced by (AI) automation driven. For example, bus drivers, light truck or delivery services drivers, heavy and tractor-trailer truck drivers, school drivers, tax drivers, travel bus drivers.

However, (AI) technology could enable some workers to focus time on other job responsibilities, boosting their productivity, and actually raised wage growth among those still holding the reshaped jobs. For example, salespeople, who currently spend a considerable amount of time driving could find themselves able to do other work when a car drives them from place to place, or inspectors and appraisers could fill out paperwork, when their car drives itself. This (AI) -driven technology should make these workers more productive, with (AI) -driven technology serving as a complement, not a substitute. New jobs will also likely be created, both in existing occupations cheaper transportation costs with lower prices and increase demand for products and all the related occupations, such as service and fulfillment, and in new occupations not currently foreseeable.

What kind of jobs will be created by (AI) technology? Predicting future job growth is extremely difficult, due to it depends on technologies or substitute for existing today as well as they may complement or substitute for existing human skills and jobs. However, (AI) will also lead to substantial indirect job creation to the degree it raises productivity and wages, it may also lead to higher consumption that would support additional jobs from high-end draft production to restaurant and retail. The future(AI) " augmented intelligence", the technology's role is as assisting and expanding the productivity of individuals rather than replacing human work. Thus, based on the biased-technical change framework, demand for labor will likely increase the most in the areas where humans complement (AI) automation technologies. For example, (AI) technology , such as IBM's Watson may improve early detection of some cancers or other illnesses, but a human healthcare professional is needed to work with patients to understand and translate patients' symptoms, inform patients of treatment options, and guide patients through treatment plans. Shipping companies may also partner workers who pick up and deliver products over the last feet with (AI) enabled autonomous vehicles that move workers efficiently from site to site. In such cases, (AI) augments what a human is able to do and allows individuals to either be move effective in their specially task or to operate on a larger scale. Thus, it seems (AI) technology will also create new jobs, raise productivities and workers' efficiencies.

Redefining management in
the workforce of artificial intelligence

2.1 Change management

(AI) will influence office administrative efficieny to be raised. In the future, due to artificial intelligence influences to some kind of human jobs nature. So, the kind of human jobs of management methods will also need to change to adapt the artificial intelligence technology input to their organizations. It will cause challenges for every executive and manager if who won't have effort to manage their teams how to apply artificial intelligence technology to work efficiently and easily. For example, division of labor will change among humans and machines will increase. Thus, companies will have to adapt their training performance and talent strategies how to emphasize on work that how to make human judgment and skills and experimentation. Thus, (IA)'s greatest impact will be on administrative coordination and control tasks, such as scheduling , resource allocation.

In fact, mangers will encounter this challenges: How to apply human experience and expertise to judge critical business decisions and practices when the information available is insufficient to suggest a successful course of action? Due to this kind of work will require new skills and mindsets. I shall indicate these change management methods to adapt (AI) technology. Such as: administration and routine tasks, scheduling , allocation of resources and reporting will fall within the intelligence machines, responsibilities that have long been reserved for humans. For example, a typical store manager or a lead nurse at a nursing home most constantly arrange shift schedules, accounting for staff members' absences owing to illness, vacation time or sudden departures.

Thus, the managers need to learn how to arrange new division of labor within the organizations after (AI) technology had been implemented to the organization. Artificial intelligence is currently influencing into once considered exclusive to humans: assessing and acting on human emotions and personality traits. The influences to managers need to change their strategies to adapt (AI) technology implements include such as below:

Firstly, managers need to spend the bulk of their time on coordination and control tasks from intelligent system implements. Their time spending on these major three aspects from impact of intelligent system: coordinate and control, solve problems and collaborate and people and community , strategy and innovation three aspects. Thus (AI) will influence managers need to change their judgment method to teach whose teams how to adapt the (AI) system operations in any organizations.

Secondly, (AI) will influence top, middle and low level management needs to change to adapt the (AI) technology operations to any owned (AI) technology organizations in the future. Intelligent machines must be trained in context. Just like humans , on-the-job training is a requirement for such machines because they typically arrive with only very general capabilities. To get the most from (AI), managers at all levels must participate in the instructional experience and in the learning process and provides managers' familiarity with such systems on these aspects, e.g. How the system works and generate advice, how the system has a proven track record , how the system provides convincing explanations , how the system can make simple rule- based decisions.

Thirdly, managers need to learn how to make judgment more accurate (AI) systems assistance. Although (AI) will invariably take on more routine work and even augment human decision-making, it won't judgment work, the application of human experience and expertise to critical business decisions when the information available is insufficient to suggest a successful course of action or reliable enough to suggest an obvious course of action. For a sense of the nature of judgment work, consider big data marketing and sales analytics. Such analytics often provide insights that can inform promotional campaigns, including predicting which promotions will generate desired sales brand further into the future, marketing executives need use judgment, combining analytics with their own and others' insight and experience.

The application of experience and expertise to critical business decisions and practice represents the real value of human judgment. But, when artificial intelligent machines are implemented to any organizations to assist the low, middle and top level management to make any business judgment. These forms of judgment work that managers can gather data interpretation, idea development more absolute from (AI) machine assistance. Thus, why these level management executives need to learn how to apply (AI) machines to help them to make any business judgment more accurate.

2.2 How (AI) influences organizational change

Consequently creative and social intelligence will be in even greater demand as (AI) makes in management and the workforce. This development will represent a long term trend in labor markets , one characterized by intensifying demand and reward for social skills with a growing desire for creative capabilities, managers will seek to fashion of ideas and hypotheses from inside and outside of the enterprise to shape solutions to their most pressing business problems. Thus, (AI) will influence overall organizational team members who have chance to participate any decision to make more accurate business judgment.

Many managers mistakenly view judgment work as only an individual discipline, failing to appreciate that it can also involve decide interpersonal and organizational practices. In more complex settings, judgment is typically a collective outcome of individuals' and teams' diverse perspectives, insights and experiences. And often , the resulting choices are better informed than decisions that an individual would have arrived at on his or her own.

Thus, when any organizations apply (AI) technology to assist managers to gather data and ideas to make any judgment. In these cases, organizations can create the conditions for effective collective judgment by establishing structures , such as " shadow advisory boards" that prompt managers and employees to source and synthesize multiple perspectives. Thus, a traditional organization (firm) might freshen its thinking is t put together a shadow advisory board, comprised of young, digital people who can apply (AI) machine assistance to make judgment work more accurate whether related to people development, problem-solving or strategizing and innovating for considerable degrees of creative and social intelligence.

Thus, on the one hand, (AI) technology machine augmentation and automation can give these advantages to human (organization managers) , e.g. developing people and community, solving problems and collaborating, coordinating and controlling work, shaping strategy and leading innovation. Besides, on the other hand, the next generation managers need have these individual attitude to treat intelligent machines to be as colleagues.

When, judgment is a human skill, intelligent machines can accelerate human learning that supports it, assisting in data -driven simulations, scenarios and search and discovery activities. Focuses on judgment work, some decisions require insight beyond what data can tell them. This is the sweet sport for human judgment, the application of experience and expertise to critical business decisions and practices. Thus, managers will also need to find ways to learn how to use digital (AI) technologies to tap into the knowledge and judgment of partners, customer external stakeholders and role models in other industries after the (AI) machine had been implemented to the organization.

Future works change:
Automation, employment
and productivity
3.1 How (AI) influences employment

Human future " micro to macro" industry trends will be affected business strategy and public policy by (AI) technology. In the future (AI) technology will influence those six themes: productivity and growth, natural resources, labor markets, the evolution of global financial markets, the economic impact of technology and innovation and urbanization. However, (AI) technology will bring economic benefits of tackling gender inequality, a new global competition, Chinese innovation and digital globalization.

Nowadays, advances in robotics artificial intelligence, and machine learning are in a new age of automation, as machines match or outperform human performance in a development to any countries. For example, automation of activities can enable businesses to improve performance by reducing errors and improving quality and speed, and in some cases achieving outcomes that go beyond human capabilities. For example, some research indicated automation could raise productivity growth globally by 0.8 to 1.4 % annually; more than 2,000 work activities across 800 occupations. When less than 5% of all occupations can be automated using demonstrated technologies about 60% of all occupations have at least 30% of constituent activities that could be automated. Many occupations will change that will be automated away: Activities most susceptible to automation involve physical activities, in highly structured and predictable environments, as well as the collection and processing of data. They are most prevalent in manufacturing , accommodation and food service and retail trade and include some middle-skill jobs. For example, such as natural language processing is a key factor. Beyond technical feasibility, the cost of technology competition with labor including skills and supply and demand dynamics, performance benefits including and beyond labor cost savings, and social and regulatory acceptance will be affected by (AI) automation technology. Thus, (AI) automation will impact to influence global employment in those aspects as below:

Firstly, assuming that people are displaced by automation will find other employment. The anticipated shift in the activities in the labor force is of a similar order as the long-term shift away from agriculture and decreases in manufacturing share of employment. Both of manufacturing and agriculture industries which would be accompanied by the creation of new types of work not foreseen at the time.

Secondly, for business, the performance benefits of automation are relatively clear. Thus, the businessmen have opportunities for their micro economies to benefits from the productivity growth potential and macro economies to benefit to encourage continued progress and innovation , investment and market incentives. At the same time, employers must innovate policies to help workers and institutions adapt to the impact on employment.

This will likely include rethinking education and training, income support and safety nets , as well as support for those dislocated, when employees need to leave themselves homes to move to other cities to learn new (AI) automation works. Thus, individuals in the workplace will need to engage move comprehensively with machines as part of their everyday activities, and acquire new skills that will be in demand in the new automation age.

Consequently , the scale of shifts in the labor force over many decades that automation technologies can be a similar order to the long -term technology -enables shifts in the developed countries' workforces away from agriculture in the 21 th century. Those shifts did not result in long-term mass unemployment because they were accompanied by the creation of new types of work not foreseen at the time. However, human will still be needed in the workforce when the total productivity gains are caused by (AI) technology.

3.2 What occupations will be influenced by (AI) technology.

In the future, scientists predict that these occupations will be influenced by (AI) technology mostly. They include : retail salespeople, food and beverage service workers, language or translation teachers, health practitioners. Since these work activities have a more relevant occupations are made up of a range of activities with different potential for (AI) automation . For example, a retail salesperson will spend more time interacting with customers, stocking shelves , or ringing up sales. Each of these activities is distinct and requires different capabilities to perform successfully.

Thus, these job activities have similar simple control characteristics. Simple activities include greet customers, answer questions about products and services, clean and maintain work areas, demonstrate product feature process sales and transactions. All these activities can have similar simple activities in order to (AI) machines can be learn how to do these activities from (AI) technology . For example, the capability perception includes sensory perception, cognitive capabilities, such as retrieving automation, recognizing known patterns( supervised learning), logical reasoning problem solving.

Thus, (AI) machine is such human, which has feeling and emotion, such as social and emotional sensing, judgement reasoning methods, natural language understanding and physical capabilities, such as mobility , navigation, gross motor skill, fine motor skills. It seems that the future, (AI) human invents machines which will have these human characteristics to do human similar behavioral job duties more easily and efficiently. It implies these above human occupations will be replaced by (AI) human invention machines in the future. Due to (AI) creation, it is possible to cause unemployment number of these above workers will increase because (AI) machines can do their similar job behavioral activities.

Consequently, employers won't need to employ many of these skillful labor. Otherwise, they can buy less number (AI) machines to attempt to do whose job activities more easily and efficiently. So, it seems (AI) machines will have more high work performance to replace these occupation workers' work performance. Finally, these occupation worker unemployment number will only increase when the (AI) machines had been invented to achieve to do their work behavioral activities absolutely success in the future.

3.3 Whether (A) technology machine labor
will replace human worker more or assist
human worker more

There is no single agreed definition of a robot how outcome of a task that is completed without human intervention. When some definitions require the task to be completed by a physical machine moves and respond to its environment, other definitions use the term robot in connection with tasks completed by software , without physical embodiment.

However, to answer the question : Whether (AI) technology machine labor will replace human worker more or assist human worker more. I shall indicate some examples to let readers to judge whether (AI) technology can create new jobs or reduce old jobs.

Firstly, I shall explain what (AI) function is. (AI) is a service robot that performs useful tasks for humans or equipment excluding industrial automation application . Thus, the classification of a robot into industrial robot or service robot is done according to its intended application. It is also a personal service robot or a service robot for personal used for a non commercial task, usually by lay persons . Examples are domestic servant robot, and pet exercising robot. It is also a professional service robot or a service robot for professional used for a commercial task, usually operated by a properly trained operator. Examples, are cleaning robot for public places, delivery robot in offices or hospitals, fire-fighting robot, rehabilitation robot and surgery robot in hospitals. Thus, these functions will be future (AI) application to our daily life necessaries or business necessaries.

However, some authors agree (AI) will bring negative outcomes of automation, due to raise competiveness, reduce human job nature. Otherwise, other authors argue (AI) will bring positive outcomes of automation, due to raise productivities, job creation, assist humans work.

On the positive outcome hand, robots can increase productivity . This is particularly important for small-to medium sized businesses both are in developed and developing countries economies. It also enables large companies to increase their competitiveness through faster product development and delivery. Increased use of robot is also enabling companies in high cost countries to re shore, or bring back to their domestic base parts of the supply chain that will have previously outsourced to sources of cheaper labor. Currently , the greater threat to employment is not a automation, but an inability to remain competitive. Automation has led overall to an increase in labor demand and positive impact on wages. The reason is that the middle-income/middle-skilled jobs have reduced as a proportion of overall contribution to employment and earnings leading to fears of increasing income inequality, the skills range within the middle income bracket is large. Thus, robots are driving an increase in demand for workers at the higher -skilled and with a positive impact on wages. This issue is how to enable middle-income earners in the lower-income range to unskilled or retain. Finally, the (AI) positive impact supporter who argue the future will be robots and humans can work together.

However, on the negative outcome hand, robots can substitute labor activities, but don't replace jobs. They believe that less than 10% of jobs are fully automatable. Increasingly , robots are used to complement and augment labor activities, the net impact on jobs and the quality of work is positive. Automation can provide the opportunity for humans to focus on higher-skilled, higher-quality and higher-paid tasks. Robots can improve productivity when they are applied to tasks that which perform more efficiently and to a higher and more consistent level of quality than humans. For example, increased productivity is enabling some firms, such as Whirlpool, Caterpillar and Ford Motors company in the US restructure their supply chains, bringing back parts of the manufacturing process to the country of origin. Thus, productivity gains due to robotics and automation are important not just at the company level, but also for build industry and nation competitiveness.

I suppose that productivity can be raised. What are the impacts of robots on employment? Firstly, the main focus of development has been on personal entertainment, which does not drive worker productivity ( manufacturing production). When the internet ( information and communication technology (ICT)) innovation. This is borne and by findings that manufacturing productivity, which has been driven by innovations in automation rather than consumer technologies, has government strongly than productivity in the services sectors of the economy in most nature economies. It seems (AI) automation will create many jobs in internet communication entertainment game industry. For example, many young people like to use internet to play any electronic games from computer or mobile at home or outside home conveniently. Thus, (AI) automation will increase demand to be invented to any new entertainment game from internet channel. It will need to employ many (AI) entertainment game inventors to create many automation entertainment games. Thus, (AI) automation in internet entertainment game industry will need human (AI) entertainment game inventors to invent the knowledge-based capital of (AI) automation entertainment games. The (AI) entertainment game inventors will need own research and development skills, form specific skills, organizational know-how skills, databased knowledge, design and various forms of intellectual property to do these (AI) automation entertainment game invention occupations in the future.

International Federation Of Robotics(2016) indicated that China will be as a major robotics manufacturer and user of robots, benefiting from jobs created by robot manufacturing and productivity gains from robot use. Chins had sold of robots to any one single market every year since 2017 year. The Chinese government has included a focus on robotics in its 10 year strategy. In order to achieve its target of a robot density of 150 units per 10, 000 workers by 2020 year. Thus, Chinese companies will have to install around 650,000 new industrial robots between 2016 to 2020 year, 2.5 times more than installed globally in 2015 year.

Hence, China (AI) manufacturing industry will need to employ many workers . It implies (AI) manufacturing industry will create many new occupations in China. Also, ministry of economy, trade and industry (2015) also showed that Japan currently has the largest stock of industrial robots in operations, primarily in the automation industry. Driven by a rapidly aging population and low productivity rates, the Japanese government has sights on a 20-fold increase in the use of robots in the non-manufacturing sector and a three-fold growth rate of labor productivity in the service sector both by 2020 year. Thus, it also implies Japan will need many robots to be provide to service industry. Due to robots will provide to serve any businessmen's clients. Thus, it is possible that the service workers won't be dismissed as well as it is depended on the serving job nature to decide whether Japan's service workers can still serve to their employer when the service (AI) robots are applied to whose employers.

Consequently, it seems that (AI) can create employment, Ministry of economy, trade and industry (2015) showed that such as China will develop the major (AI) automation manufacturing industry. The (AI) employers will need to employ many workers to manufacture any these different kinds of (AI) robots to satisfy China or overseas individual or business buyers needs. But, (AI) can also cause unemployment to the low skillful service workers. Such as if Japan some service businesses choose to buy any (AI) service robots to replace their service staffs to serve their clients. It is possible that the service staffs will be dismissed, due to (AI) robots can do such as their same service job duties to achieve better service performance.

Thus, today, it is increasingly common for people to use robots in various situations at home and in retail stores, hotels and hospitals these service industries. Robots are classified into server types based on their functionality ( service and utility robots or those designed to communicate with humans) and appearance ( humanoid robots or mechanical robots). The type of robot, to which each country allocated particular importance in the advance of robotics, reflects the sense of values and preferences of its population. Thus, if the country has high population needs to use robots, then they will influence either more new jobs creation or more old job loss in the country's (AI) manufacturing or (AI) service industries both. For example, Japan respondents often associate the term " robot " with humanoid robots that can communicate with human and they have a high level of familiarity with robot. The US has the highest level of robot utilization at home and in retail stores with its people being the most enthusiastic about the future use of robots. Germany shows a strong tendency to consider robots for industrial purposes and its people feel strong effort to the presence of robots in their households.

In conclusion, to judge whether how (AI) will influence the country's employment to be better or worse. It will depend on the country home buyers (users) or business buyers (users) how to use (AI) for their daily needs. If the country , such as US retail stores need to use (AI) , it will have possible to reduce some or many retail service workers. Even, if the country , such as Japan has many home users need to use (AI) , it will not influence the employment market. Otherwise, it will raise (AI) salespeople numbers. Even, if the country, such as Germany and China will have many (AI) manufacturers, then it will create many (AI) manufacturing occupations for these (AI) manufactory workers. Consequently, (AI) robots manufacturing and service needs will have positive or negative impact to any country's employment. It will depend on the (AI) service provision and service workers' job nature as well as the manufacturing workers of (AI) knowledge level to decide their employment chance in their country's employment market.

## 3.4 Robot society advantages and disadvantage

Our technology had been developing to (AI) artificial intelligent or robot social development stage. When one day, global has many jobs are replaced to do by robots, e.g. cleaners, cookers, drivers, customer servicers, hotel food service delivers etc. general social simple tasks are replaced by robots. Can our societies are dominated by robots? Is it possible that our societies can be dominated when global has manyjobs are replaced by robots? Why can our societies be dominated when many robots can replace humans to do ourselves future simple jobs , even complex jobs? Can robots bring positive or negative social impacts when we have many jobs can be replaced by robots? I shall attempt to explain whether our future societies will be become to improve better or worse when we have many jobs are replaced by robots as below:

In traditional societies,when our societies had not invented this kind thing of (AI) or robot technological tools to serve our societies or help us to do any simple or even complex tasks in our societies. Our social labour number needs must be increased, e.g. restaurant cookers, shopping center cleaners, shopping center customer service, hotel food delivery, office or appartment securities, warehouse logistic transport, even public transport tool drivers. They may be repplaced by robots easily in future.

Hence, in our future societies, many simple jobs or low skillful level of occupations may be replaced by robots, when robots can be taught to learn how to do our simple tasks in our future societies. Hence, when any one of these low skillful occupations can be replaced by robots. In our societies, these low skillful or low educational level workers their employers' need number may be influenced to reduce. Otherwise, due to robots have these advantages, e.g. non negative emotion, laze, 24 working hours, or none sleeping need, none hungry feeling or none lunch or dinner time need, none salary expenditure. So, future our societies need robots to replace human to do any low educational level or low skillful level of simple jobs number will be influenced by robot advantages factor. The question concerns whether robots may dominate ourfuture societies if our future has many simple jobs can be replaced by robots.

How can robots dominate our future social tasks to do ? Can they bring advantages if they can dominate to do our social future many simple jobs? Firstly, we need to ensure that when our societies has many simple tasks which can be replaced by robots, then our societies will have many simple jobs or occupations may be influenced to disappear due to many employers will decide to dismiss their low skillful or low educational level stafs, they will buy many robots to help them to do these simple jobs in their organizations, e.g. hotels can apply robots to do food delivery tasks or cleaning rooms tasks, or hotel securities tasks, or opening hotel front doore tasks or the hotel restaurent can apply robots to do cooking tasks or food delivery tasks , shopping centers can apply robots to do customer service tasks. So, it seems that any hotels may apply robots to replace human workers to do any hotel service simple jobs. It means that hotels may dismiss many low skillful workers and robots can replace these service workers to do their tasks easily. Also, any organizational warehouses departments can apply robots to do goods transport or delivery tasks, so it seems that any warehouse logistic worker transport tasks which can be replaced by robots. SO, future there are many warehouses do not need logistic transport workers, they can be replaced by robots. Consequently, many of these organizational tasks will be replaced by robots or these low skillful or low educational level occupations will be influenced to disappear by robots.

IN fact, in long term, any organizations spend to robots expenditure which must lower to compare to spend to employees wages expenditure. Instead of reducing organizational cost beneficial aspect, robots will not have laze, hungry, sleeping need, demand increasing wage needs or negative emotional feeling to compare human workers. So, in future, general social simple tasks may be influenced to reduced or replaced by robots. When many organizations begin to accept robots to replace human to do simple tasks to serve themselves organizations. It seesm that robots will have effort to dominate our future organizational efficiency or future organizational service performance, because many employers begin to evaluate performance to robots more than humen workers, they begin to compare whether robots can perform better or worse to compare human workers, when robots may be applied to work with human workers in teams together. For example, when the hotel applies robots to help hotel room cleaners to clean all hotel rooms. The hotel needs to evaluate whether the robot's cleaning effort is better or worse to compare human hotel cleaners or the restaurants needs to apply robots to cooperate to human cookers to cook any kinds of foods to give clients to eat in team together. The restaurant needs to evaluate whether the robots can cook better taste of foods to let clients to feel to eat or worse taste of foods to let clients to feel to eat. So, this restaurant needs to evaluate whether these cooking robots their cooking skills are better or worse to compare human cookers.

Hence, future many business organizations need to evaluate robots their service performance or working skills or efficiency to in order to decide whether their task efforts are better or worse to compare human employees. If they believe that robots their tasks efforts or service performance or efficiencies are improved or better to compare humans, then robots have possible to be applied to dominated the overall team tasks in any organizations. So, it seems that future robots have possible to dominate any organizational overall team tasks if the organization feels robots their performances are improved to be better to compare human workers.

On consequence, when the organization has many simple tasks are dominated by robots, the organization won't need to employ many managers to supervise employees' tasks any teams, because many of simple tasksa re replaced to do by robots. Organizations only need to spend time to arrange whether the robot needs how to do the kind of simple tasks e.g. for hotel organizations example, it only needs to teach robots how to clean the hotel room, how to deliver foods to client rooms, how to cook good taste of foods in the hotel restaurant kitchen. Because robots do not need to be supervise, they only need to taught to learn how to do the kind of simple tasks, when they can be taught to learn how to do the kind of simple tasks to serve the organization. Then, they follow the "computer program instruction" to finish the kind of simple tasks daily. Consequently, the organization must not need to employ managers or supervisors to supervise robot performance or working behaviors in order to evaluate their performance whether they can satisfy client individual need or organizational internal working needs. So, it means that instead of the low skillful workers, robots may replace managers or supervisors positions in any organizations, when they can be applied to dominate to do the organization;s overall any simple tasks to achieve the best performance daily.

Reference
International Federation Of Robotics, 2016. IFR press release world robotics

report. IFR, org . 29 Sept. Accessed Feb. 01, 2017. http://www.ifr.org/news/ifr-press-release/world-robitics report -2016-8321.

Ministry of economy, trade and industry, Japan, 2015, Japan's robot strategy. Ministry of economy, trade and industry.

# EIGHT

# HOW HUMAN BEHAVIOR INFLUENCES ROBOT NEEDS

Human Behavioral network job brings social economic benefits

What does human network job mean ? Why may human network job be popular? Why human network job behavior may influence economy ? Nowadays internet is popular to use. We can apply internet to find data , search any new things, even earn money. Why does internet may become huma network job source. For example, e-publish may be one kind of new human network job. Any authors may apply internet channel to help them to sell electronic or paper books from e-publisher web store. They may apply facebook, you tub etc. any online channel to promote themselves new books to let new readers to know whether when they may buy themselves favourable new topic books to read from electronic publisher web store.

Thus, future electronic publisher industry may help any authors to build internet network platform to help them to sell and promote ot advertise their any one new electronic or paper book topic to let global any one reader to choose to buy their any new topic books from electronic publisher web store easily and conveniently. However, it implies that electronic network platform author may be one kind of future new human network job in our societies.

How electronic network platform author job may bring economy benefit in macro economy view? A person can have few friends, contacts and still be very influential if these few

friends and contacts are themselves highly influential, e.g. one author must not need to know any one reader in global society. When they like to choose any electronic books from electronic internet network platform. They may become the author's any one topic book buyer, when they feel the author's any one topic book is fun and attract they make decision to buth the strange author whose the topic book from electronic book publisher's platform web store conventiently in short time. Although, they are strangers, they do not know themselves , but the reader can understand what it way that made Google from writing platofrm to create new creative mind and typing network job method to replace traditional hand writing book method for global authors. It will be one kind of new human network writing job.

Hence, global any one reader can apply an innovative search engine , such as google.com to find whether whom author personal new topic books are value to read from internet.

Then, the electroniuc publisher's web store may be new book store platform sale network to help the author to sell many electronic or paper books from electronic network platform

in short time. So, internet may be future new network plaform to help global any one author to create network writing job absolutely. Furthermore, internet may be popular social media

to help any one author to build goold relationship between his/her readers. It is one kind of new network, human network job. New authors do not need to buy many paper books to prepare to put in any one book shop warehouse. Their every book can print on demand to reduce out of book stock in any one book shop. They may choose to sell either electronic books or paper books both from any one book publisher web store. So, electronic network platform may be one kind of good writing channel to help human authors to create income and it can also help authors to bring new creative mind and new topic fun content books to let readers to know and buy to read from electronic publisher network platform.

Why does human behavior may be one kind of new human network job to bring global economic advantages. ALthough, it may be free income or without inocme, but the person does the network behavior, his/her behavior may be bring advantages to influence many other people's health. For this case, when a worker in a coffee shop in an airport gets a vaccination aganinst the flu, it does not only helps him or her stay healthy, but also helps the many travellers who might otherwise have been inflected if that workers caught the flu. So, the externality , the result implies the vaccination of even a part of a community conveys benefits to the whole community. For example, governments pay special attention to the vaccinations of school children, teachers, health mothers, and the elderly, categories of people particularly susceptible not only to catching, but also to transmitting a disease.

It is not accidental that governments are heavily involved with vaccination . When there are externalities, free market, fail to persuade individual incentives with society's
their the worker's decision of whether to get a vaccine ends up attracting whether other people get sick. The workers might not fully take all these other people's potential suffering into account when making her or his vaccination decision.

As Stanford University does many suggestions, understand this and tries to help them make the right decisions and so providers free flu vaccines for its staff and students.
Small pockets of unvaccinated individuals can allow a disease to gain a spread more widely well-being. For example, parent weighing the costs and benefits of a vaccine for their child is not always thinking of the consequences of that vaccination to other people. THese are markets in which subsidizing or regulating behavior can make everyone better off. Because the reason for requiring that a child be vaccinated before enrolling in school is not just to protect that child, because each child's vaccination affects others via potential contagions.

Robots take our jobs behavioral and economy influences

Robot job behavior brings economy influences


If one day robots can replace human to do simple, even complex jobs. They will bring what influences to our global societial economy.The popular economic refrain declares that the
global middle class is dying and robots will soon take our jobs, e.g. shopping center customer service jobs, library service jobs, cinema ticket sale jobs, restaurant kitchen cooker jobs,
even, bus drivers, taxi drivers etc. public transport driving jobs, accountant, doctors etc. professional jobs. Whether it is beautiful or petty matter if our future societies have many human jobs can be replaced to do from robots.

Businessman must may reduce to employ employees and reduce to pay salary or wage, when robots can be replaced to do their employees tasks. But, societies must bring unemployement rate rises , due to societies will have many people loss jobs when their employers choose to buy robots to serve their clients or do any office tasks or customer service or cleaning etc. tasks.

In micro economy view, employers may save money in long term, but in macro economy view, it will cause unemployment ratio rises , even crime rate rises when there are many people lose

jobs in societies. These models of doom, though, fail to account for the hundreds of businesses riding the waves of change in their industries when robots may be invented to replace human to do many simple , even complex tasks in our future societies.

WE may image that one small factory needs to manufacture fishes canes to sell to supermarket, the small , cheaper stuff and higher margin parts of the fishes manufacture industry. Before, this factory needs to employe many human factory workers need to help every fresh customer makeing the perfect fishing gear, designed for performance, durability, and cost in order to achieve to manufacture every fish cane in whole fished processing manufacturing stages. Every worker needs to spend about 15 to twenty minutes to finish every fish cane , till to delivery to any supermarket to sell. If this fish canes manufacturing factory can apply manufacturing robots to help them to finish any one working tasks , every robot can only spend five minutes to finish whole fresh fish cane manufacturing process. Thus, every robot can

help this factory save 10 to 15 minutes time to finsh every fish cane manufacturing process. IN fact, time is money, because when every robot can help this factory to reduce 10 to 15 minutes time to compare human worker. Then, this factory can finish about 20 fish canes in one hour if it can use robot to help it to manufacture fish canes. Otherwise, if this factory still use human workers to help it to manufacture fish canes, then it can finsh about 3 to 4 fish canes in one hour. SO, the manufacturing efficiency ensures that robots must help this fish manufacturing factory to raise fish canes number more than human workers. So, in robotic behavioral economy view, manufacturing robots must help this fish canes manufacturing factory to raise fish canes manufacturing number and deliver increasing number to supermarkets to prepare to sell every day. Robots can help this fish canes manufacturing factory bring manufacturing time saving, rising manufacturing efficiency, improving performance and reducing wages expenditure long time advantages in micro economy view. However, manufacturing robots can also bring disadvanages to society, e.g. increasing unemployment ratio, increasing crime rate,

this factory workers will lose jobs and income, they need earn social welfare from government and increasing government finance pressure in short time, even long time in macro economic view.

Stanford University graduate program in economics, Scott lecturer explained that "in demand and supply economic theory for robots supply and demand case, robots supply number increasing may influence human workers demand number decrease. It sometimes calls " the efficient frontier".

No specific human beings were mentioned in any of economics classes. As robots supply and demand in market case, They ( robots) may be purely theoretical " agents" who reached to the most reasonable sale prices in order to persuade any one businessman buyer to make manufacturing robot buying decision whether robots can help him / her to bring how much saving time , saving money, saving cost, improving performance, efficiency economic benefit before he/she plans to reduce workers number when he/she decides to apply robots to replace human workers in his/her factory or office or any service department, e.g. cinema ticket sale service, shopping center customer service, shopping center cleaning , supermarket customer service etc. service or sale tasks. When robots can replace human to do any one of these tasks in any organizations. So, robots may be human worker agents who reached to prices the way robots would react to a software

command. There was nothing that explained why some people thrived and others did n't or why truly brilliant, hardworking people could fail when much lazier folks succeeded." Having been admitted to the Stanford University graduate program in economics, Scott lecturer hoped to get his answers there.

How robots influence our future social changing? Using the right technology can be a boon to your business in this economy. For internet example, it is easier than ever to find well-matched customers all around the world, to stay in contact with them, and to more quickly design the products they want. If you focus solely on being cutting -edge, though you risk letting the technology

take over what should be very robust relationships with your customers , employees, and colleagues. IN nowaddays society, technoligical advances and cutomation, personal

relationships in business are more crucial than ever. I mean that robots can not replace human to serve clients to let them to feel more comfortable and passion more easily. For shoe shop case example, if the shoe shop apply one robot to serve its clients to replace human shoe salesperson to serve its shoe customers. Robots ensure that they can not persuade every shoe potential buyer to make shoe buying decision more easily when robots need to contact every shoe potential buyer. The reason is simple, because robots can not touch any one shoe buyer individual emotion very easier.

If the shoe buyer needs the robots to help him/her to choose any right shoe styles when he/she can not feel himself / herself can make the most right shoe style choice decision. The robots can not replace human shoe salesperson to make shoe style choice judgement more easily. They must need longer time to analyze whether which shoe style may be the most suitable to the shoe buyer. Otherwise, human shoe salesperson may attempt to make the most right shoe style choice decision to help any one shoe buyer to chooce the most right style shoe because he/she owns shoe style sale experience, shoe style knowledge, the most important reason is that they can feel every shoe customer individual emotion to touch whether he/she will feel comfortable or happy when they attempt to help every shoe customer to seek the most right shoe style in every shoe customer whole shoe searching processing. Othwerwise, serving robots are only one machine, they can not touch or feel every shoe customer individual emotion whether he/she feel comfortable or unhappy or happy when they need to contact them in whole shoe searching processing. Hence, I believe that some tasks robots can

not repalce human staff to do very easily. Otherwise, robots may bring disadvanatges to let any one businessman to loss his/her customers, due to robots can not touch every customer

emotion to compare human staff in service tasks more easily. Robots serving customer behaviors may cause money lose and customers number lose to the shop in micro economic view.

Intellectual human economic behaviors

What does intellectual human economic behaviors mean ? I believe that when we choose or decide to do intellectual behaviors, then our societies will be influenced to bring economic growth in consequence.I shall attempt to indicate pollution case to explain how and why eithet our intellectual or foolish behaviors may bring economic growth or recession in consequence as below:

On one hand, for air pollution social case aspect example, if we only consider to buy cars to drive for working aimr or holiday leisure aim. Then, our societies air will be polluted. Our health will be influenced to bad. Our car driving behaviors may cause global environment air pollution serously. In long tiem, global air pollution will bring our bodies health to be bad. Although, ourselves car driving behaviors may bring our driving travelling leisure enjoyment and comfortable feeling in short time, also we so not need to pay public transport fare often, but we need to compensate ourselves health economic intangible loss due to air pollution , when cars number increases, dirty air will cause ouselves health to become bad.

In the result, we will need to pay more medical expenditure when we are old age, due to ourselves bodies will become bad, due to we breathe global dirty air every day, due to ourselves cars pollute air in long time, e.g. 10 to 20 years, even 30 more without limited air pollution environment. So, driving cars behavior may be one kind of human foolish behavior and our foolish behavior may bring ourselves future long time medical expenditure absolutely.

One the other hand, water pollution social aspect, if we often keep much rubblish to pollute sea, oil exploration porcessing pollute ocean , ships gas pollute ocaen, then fishes will eat polluted food and drive dirty water, due to global ocean is polluted.

In fact, because human only to conside how to buy boats to carry on leisure enjoyment activities, or catch cruises to travel on the sea. Also, oil manufacturers only consider researching anywhere to find new oil exploration places to manufacture oil product, when their oil exploration processes pollute ocarn . Consequently, global fishes drink polluted warer or eat polluted food. They will have poison. SO, human will have high chance to eat poison polluted fishes, due to fishes are poison or are polluted.

So, human is doing foolish activities, we only hope to find oil exploration places to pollute ocean or we only spend money to buy ticket to catch ships to travel anywhere in global ocean. All of these human foolish behaviors will bring pollution to global ocean. On consequently, we will need to compensate to eat polluted or dirty or poision fishes, ourselves bodies health will be bad. In long time, we need have high chance to pay medical expenditure when we are old. So, pollution case may be one good example to explain how and why human foolish behavior may influence ourselves future need to compensate serious medical loss.

All of these human foolish behavior will bring pollution to global ocean. On consequently, we will need to compensate to eat polluted or dirty or poison fished , ourselves bodies health will be bad. In long time, we will have high chance to pay medical expenditure, when we are old. So, pollution case may be one good example to explain how and why human ourselves intellectual or foolish behaviors may influence future long time economic loss or economic growth or recession in micro and micro economic view.

On another water pollution aspect hand, if we often keep rubbish to sea, oil exploration processing pollutes ocean and ships' gas pollute ocean, then fishes will eat polluted food and drink dirty water, due to fishes will eat polluted food and drink dirty sea water because the global ocean is polluted seriously.

In fact, because human only consider how to buy boats to carry on any leisure water activities, or catches cruises to travel on the sea. Also, oil manufacturers only consider any where to find oil exploratin places to manufacture oil products from ocean, when their pol exploration processes can plooute ocean. Consequently, global fishes drink polluted water or eat direty food. They will have poison. So, human will have high chance to eat poison fishes.

Otherwise, such as pollutin case, it can infuence inflation or deflation. Consequently, the reason indicates supply and demand theory. If air pollution is serious, then we will consider health issue, global cars demand number may be influenced to reduce, when global cars number demand will reduce, global car prices and supply number will need to change to fall down in order to attract or persuade global car consumers choose to make car purchase decision.

Hence, global car manufacture number and car price will be influenced to reduce, due to global air pollution issue. Consequently, deflation will occur because when the country citizen usually does not spend much extra saving money to buy car expensive goods. Money value will be low. Otherwise, if global cair pollution is not serious, human considers to buy cars to enjoy driving leisure lives. So, global car demand is influenced to increase , also global car price will also influenced to increase.

Consequently, gobal human will choose to buy cars to drive. Due to we accept to spend extra saving to buy expensive car goods. Car sale price and supply may be influenced to rise up. Money value is influenced to reduce. Inflation may be influenced, due to global car consumers number increases, we would not have extra money to spend easily. Car expensive goods expenditure influences our spending habit to avoid to make car purchase decision more easily. So, human intellectual or foolish activities may bring inflation or deflation consequency in possible indirectly in macro economic view.

On conclusion, above pollution case explain that how and why human intellectual or foolish economic behaviors may bring inflation or deflation consequency as wll as economic growth or recession consequency as well as any goods demand and supply increasing or decreasing consequency. It implies that human behavior may have indirect relationship to influence any goods demand and supply number to either increase or decrease result as well as any goods price will be influenced to increase or decrease in micro and macro economic view.

The relationship between social change and human behavior

Why does economic changes may influence human individual behavioral change? I shall attempt to indicate shopping behavior and staying at home behavior to explain their case and effect relationsip as below:

Human behavior can be influenced by economic change or economic change can be influenced by human behavior? Why does recession may influence consumers reduce shopping desire? In social recession suitation, it is possible that many people lose jobs suddenly, due to businessmen lose many customers. They need to make decision to reduce employees number in order to continue to keep businesses. Consequently, many firms ( organizations) their employees may lose jobs. When they have much time, due to lose jobs, they will feel to avoid to spend too much time and money to go to shopping often. Many losing jobs people, they will often stay at homes. So, they will reduce time to go to shopping, then non essential products won't their preferable choice purchase products. Hence, recession will change many losing jobs people their shopping or consumption desires to avoid to buy non essential products often . Usually when economic boom, many people have jobs to do because consumers number must increase when many people have jobs to do. Then, many people can accept to spend money to buy non essential products often. Many people feel spend time to go to shopping can satisfy their purchase of any kinds of new products useful psychology or desire. So, recession is one good example to explain it can influence many people do not like often to leave homes to go to shopping easily. Many people like to stay at homes, becaue they feel worry about spending too much shopping time when they leave homes. Their staying home time is one good negative shopping behavior example. So, economic change may influence human individual behavior changes , they have direct cause and efect relationship in behavioral economic view.

May human behavior influence economic change? Is it possible that human behavior may bring the country social economic change in macro economic or micro behavioral economic view ? I shall indicate publishing industry example. Do you feel that if there are many students feel learning is very important when they read many books or many of students feel interesting to read or they have reading new books in habit, then it is possible that the country will have many students like to spend time to go to any book shops to choose the books, they feel that they can help they learn new knowledge. Then the country will increase students number, they often spend time to visit any one book shop every week. Their visiting book shops behavior which may become their habits. So, the country will increase students number, they often spend time to visit book shops. Also, it implies that visiting book shops behaviors may be their behavioral habits.

So, when the country has many students often spend time to visit book shops , their visiting book shops behaviors may help any one book shop to raise books sale chance. So, the country's student individual often visiting book shop behaviors, their habitual visiting book shops behaviors must may assist help any one book shop to increase books sale number absolutely.

Consequently, any one book shop , its books sale bumber must be influenced to increase to increase because the country will have many students like or feel need visit book shops habit in order to choose any suitable books to buy to read at home in order to raise themselves learning effort. When the country has many bok shops often have many students visit their book shops, then their books sale number may be influenced to increase. It explain why student individual visiting book shop behavior may help any one book shop sale number increases also.

How human productive behavior may influence economic development

May any country which citizen behavior assist themselves country development? It is one cause and effect economic question. I mean that if the country itself citicen can not concentrate mind or energy to choose to do one kind of industry in order to let themselves country can bring the most benefit, then whether the counry itself economy can bring the most serious economic benefit. I shall attempt to indicate these countries themselves indistry choice to explain whether these countries themselves citizen productive behavior may help themselves countries to achieve the largest economic benefits. I shall indicate as below:

New Zealand farmer individual wine productive behavior

For New Zealand country example, this country concerns itself effort is foucs on farming agricultural aspect. So, this country has many farmers concentrate on farming agricultural aspect. May New Zealanders choose to spend time to produce different kinds of wines, e.g. wine or red grape wine is for the people are eating meat, or they are eating dinner.

When these New Zealanders their behaviors choose to do farming or agriculture to grow and produce different kinds of taste of white or red grape wine drinking products job. Themselves grape agriculture behavior will influence these New Zealanders themselves, they can learn how to improve different kinds of grape wine drinking products in order to achieve every kinds of white or read grape wines taste improving aim during their white or red grape producing process.

Why can New Zealander every individual white or read grape wine producers improve their white or read grape wine taste more easily? In behavioral economic view, it can explain that why any one New Zealander white or read grape wine producer can be encouraged or excited or persuaded to concentrate nervous and energy and effort to learn how to improve their white or red grape wine products easily.

In fact, New Zealand is one agricultural food export country. It has good natural environment resource , e.g. land, seed to provide any one farmer to produce themselves any kinds of agricultrual food products, e.g. fruit, or wine food products. Because New Zealanders know themselves country has enough natural resource . So, in common, many New Zealanders choose to attempt to do farming agricultural jobs in order to export themselves any kinds of fruit or meat or wine products to overseas or sell to domestic in order to earn profit.

So, when these New Zealand farmers number has been increasing every year. This country farmers will feel themsleves competition between this New Zealand farmers themselves are serious due to they may feel New Zealanders choose to do agriculture businesses in order to export themselves different kinds of farming food to overseas or sell to local to earn profit.

Hence, when many New Zealand farmers feel that farmers number has been increasing every year. They will feel themselves competition is serious. They must need to spend much time and nervous and effort to research what method is the best how to produce the best taste of white or red grape wine products in order to let local or overseas wine buyers to choose to buy his/ her producing white or read grpae products to drink.

Hence, in competition psychological view, may influence many New Zealand white or reaad wine producers had been beginning to change their learning behavior on researching what method is the best in order to produce the best quality of taste red or white wine products to sell in order to attract overseas or local white or read grape wine drinkers to choose to buy his/her wine products. Their behavior will focus on learning how to raising or improving white or read grape wine taste method more than only focus on producing a large number white or red grape wine products. They believe wine quality is more important to compare wine producing number. So, New Zealand wine producers themselves wine producers behaviors have been changing on concentrating on researching wine quality method aspect more then wine producing number aspect in behavioral economic view.

America high technological productive behavior

For America example, US is one high technological country, it owns many high technological knowledge talent inventors, e.g. computer science inventors. Hence, US must attract many diferent countries owning high technological computer inventors choose to go to US to develop their computer science profession career. Also, it seems that when many computer science inventors or professions choose to go to US to develop themselves computer science new career. In behavioral economic view, due to their leaving themselves countries choice, which may bring influence themselve country job behaviors need to be changed. They must need to adapt US new live. Because they will forgive their past computer science job. These computer science professionals need to spend time to adapt US new lives. They " past computer science job behaviors" will need to be changed to their new US any computer employer's new computer science job model.

Because their traditional computer science jobs needed to be forgot in their themselves countries. They will feel their old computer science job knowledge and behavior needed to change in order to let their US any one new of computer company employer feels satisfactory to accept their new working behavior in any one US computer organization.

So, on the other hand, many US computer company employer will feel that they must need time to accept any one new overseas computer science professions their working behaviors, their working attitude daily, because these foreign comouter science professional, their past computer working behaviors and working attitude must be different to US domestic computer science professions.

In behavioral economic view, these overseas computer science professions, their working behaviors and attitude must be needed to change in order to adapt any one US new computer company itself domestic or local computer science professional stafs themselves daily working behaviors and attitude because these overseas and local computer science professionals must need to team work together.

In behavioral economic view, it is only one way that foreign computer science professionals must need to change themselves past country traditiona daily working behaviors and attitude in order to cooperate with these US local computer science professionals in teams more easily.

Consequently, if these foreign compute science professionals can change their past working behaviors and attitude to let any one US local computer science professional feels to cooperate with them easily in short time. Then, the US computer company itself whole computer professional teams themselves efficiencies will be influenced to raised or improved by the changing past working attitude and working behaviors of these foreign computer science professionals. So, in behavioral economic view, only if US any one computer company hopes itself computer teams themselves efficiency can be raised or improved when it decides to employ foreign computer science professionals and US domestic computer science professionals. They need to work in teams together. They must need to let these foreign computer science professionals to know how to change their working behaviors and attitude to let their domestic computer science professionals feel easy to work together. Then, the US computer company itself whole team efficiency must be rasied or improved easily in short time.

● China share market investing behavior

For China share market example, economic development depends on financial market. Because if many Chinese have interest to invest to carry on shares buying and selling activities in orde to learn how to earn shares interest and share profit when the China shareholder can make decision to sell himself/herself shares in the the high price, then he/she can earn money when he/she can sell the China company's shares in the high sale share price position.

If China has many Chinese like to spend time to carry on investing shares activities. Themselves shares buying and selling behaviors will influence China has many companies can increase fund from many Chinese shareholders in order to have enough money to expand or develop themselves businesses in China in long term.

Consequently, when China can have many Chinese like to attempt to carry on buying and selling shares investing behaviors in China share market. Themselves buying and selling shares behaviors can help many Chinese companies have effort to increase enough money or capital in order to continue to do their businesses in long term absolutely. So, it explains why when many Chinese become shareholders , they can assist China will have many companies continue to develop their businesses if many Chinese like to carry on shares buying and selling investing behaviors in long time in China financial investment market nowadays in behavioral economic view.

Why has any individual country have many people invest share behavior which can influence the country's macro consumption desire?

I shall apply shares market buying and selling investment behavior to explaiin why shares investment behavior which may impact the country's overal consumption desire as below:

In behavioral economic view, I assume that when the coutry has many people have interest to attempt to carry on shares buying and selling investment behavior, then their frequent shares buying and selling behaviors which may bring negactive consumption desire or shopping desire of these shares investors their consumer behavior.

The reason is simple, when the country has many share buyers number suddenly been increasing rapidly. Consequently, these large group share investors must need to spend much time to research any kinds of company shares variations, whether when their share prices will rise up of fall down in order to achieve buying the company's shares in the lowest price and selling the company's shares in the highest price level in order to earn profit. Basic on this reason, they must need to spend much extra time to research share prices changing behavior every day, e.g. one working person will wait to leave his/her job, after he/she can spend time to gather data to research the day's share price changing behavior after dinner. So, the working person's right time may be his/her share price market research behavior. Before he/she may spend his/her night time to go to shopping after dinner, but nowadays, he/she will fogive to do his/her shopping behavior before dinner or after dinner at hight sometime. He/she will make decision to spend much night time to turn on computer to click on share market website to research his/her share purchase choice to investigate whether his/her share price whether it rises up or falls down at the moment in order to make his/her share buying or selling decision at ever night time.

I mean the when the country has many people are share investors, their shares investment behavioral spenging time which will influence many shops lose customers at might often because the country will have many people feel need to spend night time to turn on computer or watch television to investigate share price variation. So, the country will have many people / share investors choose to stay at home in order to carry on share price variation investigation behavior, they need to listen share market update news from radios or watch the share market update news from computer or TV at home every night. Consequenly, they must reduce times to leave themselves homes at night. So, their shopping behavior also will be reduced. Because these share investors feel need to spend time to investigate share price variation news at homes which can bring economic benefits ( high opportunity benefits) when they choose to forgive to leave homes to go to shopping times ( opportunity cost) every night.

On conclusion, it seems that when the country has many people are share investors, then their share price investigating behavior may bring negative shopping emotion at night. Consequently, the country's any one shop may lose many customers from this share investor consumer group in behavioral economic view. Hence, when the country's share investors number had been increasing rapidly, it will influence any shops lose many customers from this share investing customer group at night frequenly in short time, even long time in behavioral economic view, because their shopping desires or shopping emotion will be brought negative feeling when they make decisions to spend much time to listen radios or watch TV or computers share price update nes at night. Hence, share market will bring negative impact to influence consumer shopping desire or negative shopping emotion in behavioral economic view.


Can technology influence human shopping behavioral change?
Nowadays, technological development has reached mature stage, whether technological mature stage may bring positive or negative shopping emotion influence to global consumers. I shall aplly internet inventin or ecommerce shopping channel tool to explain whether internet technology can bring postive or negative influence to global consumer behavior in behavioral economic view.
Internet is a good technological tool, it brings e-commerce business chance. In fact, commonly, global has have many businessmen choose to use internet channel to carry on their products transactions between global

online-buyers and their electronic websites. So, global many shoppers had begun to feel online shopping is more convenient to compare visiting shops shopping. Their shopping behaviors have been changed from internet technological tool. Global has many shoppers choose to buy any products from any overseas or local businessmen their web stores. They only need to spend time to find any businessmen their webstores to choose the most suitable products to pay visa to buy from their webstores. at homes. So, in general, global had have may shoppers had changed their shopping behaviors from visiting shops to visiting webstores at homes often.

So, it seems that internet technological tool had influenced global many shops disappear, but internet webstores will be replaced their actual shops on streets. Some of businessmen either they choose webstores to replace shops or choose websotes and shops both or still keep shops only. Hence, internet tool influences global businessmen have three kinds of products sale channels to let globa local and overseas consumers to choose how to buy their products.

However, in fact, many of global shoppers, youngers and olders had begun to accept to buy any products from webstores. They feel to spend time to leave homes to visit shops , their shopping behaviors will be wasted time to not essential part to their daily lives. Hence, since internet technological invention, it had changed many consumers their traditional visiting shops shopping habit to change to buying products from webstores channel.

However, on the one hand, internet creates webstores ecommerce shopping channel to let global many consumers do not need to leave homes to go to shopping. It brings negative visiting shops shopping emotion to global general consumers nowadays. But on the other hand, it also brings positive visiting internet webstores shopping emotion to global general consumer nowadays. So, it seems that global many consumers feel that they often do not need to spend much time to go out shopping. Many global consumers feel convenient and enjoy to choose any products to buy from different internet webstores, when the online buyer chooses the most suitable product, he she only needs to pay visa card to buy the product from the online seller's webstore conveniently at home.

Hence, online shopping can bring economic benefit to online buyers, e.g. avoiding walking time or spending transport fare to visit the shop to go to shopping, shortening or reducing shopping time to do another important matter.

On conclusion, global many consumers began feel online shopping can bring more economic benefits on shortening shopping time, avoiding transport fare spending aspect. So, online shopping will be popular shopping behavior for future long time. It may encourage global many shoppers can make rapid shopping decision in short time in order to carry on any products buying transaction to global any one online shopper in short time easily in behavioral economic view. So, global many businessmen had begun to build themselves one attraction webstore in order to persuade different countries consumers to choose to click themselves webstores from internet channel to buy any kinds of products in short time easily.

So, internet technology had changed consumers traditional shopping behaviors to build positive online shopping emotion as well as raise online sellers' any products sale chance easily in behavioral economic view.

Why and how human behavior may influence the country's economic growth or recession?

When one country has many people choose to do the same matter for one period, whether their behavior may influence the country's pvera; economic growth or recession . I shall attempt to indicate cases toexplain their relationship as below:

For flowing rubblish behavioral case example, do you feel that when the country has many people often flow rubblish on the streets, instead of their flowing rubblish behavior may bring streets dirty? But, their flowing rubblish behavior may explain that this country has people may have enough money to buy food to ear, or enough cloths to wear, enough bottles of water to drink, even they may have enough money to buy new television, radio, refrigeraters , washing machines, desktops or laptops electronic home products from old to new to use in order to satisfy their living needs. So, when they flow old electronic home products, their flowing old home electronic products behaviors may seem that they have enough money to buy other new home electronic products to replace old home electronic products to use at homes.

However, it seems thaat this country ought have many people have jobs to do. So, many of them, they can easy to make purchase decison to flow any old home electronic products and buy any new home electronic products to use . Because this country has many people have jobs to do. So, they can often not use old home electonic products to become rubblishs to flow on streets after they had bought any kinds of new home electronic homes.

In fact, it also implies that this country's economy grows rapidly. So, many businesses can glow up rapdly. When they expanded their businesses, they must need to increase employees number in order to let they help themselves to raise productivity or serve their clients absolutely. So, when the country has many businesses can grow up, it seems that its economy must be better or it is improved to compare past. Due to many different kinds of home electronic products had been often bought to use by this country people in this period. So, this country's any streets can be observed that expensive electronic home products were flowed on streets anywhere. then, this country will have many electronic home products sellers can sell their home electronic products very easily. When this country has many people can find any kinds of jobs to do easily. So, due to unemploymen rate had been decreasing.

In behavioral economic view, as this many electronic home products rubblish country case, we can observe this country may have many people have jobs to do. So, consumption number has been increased long time. So, cheap food, or expensive home electronic products may be rubblish on any streets. This country's people , their flowing rubblish behaviors may be explained that many of people have enough jobs to do, so they have ability to buy any good taste food to eat or buy any kinds of expensive electronic home products to use. So, this country's economy may be improved for this long period. So, in behavioral economic view, when this country can have many electronic home products rubblishs are flowed on anywherer in streets frequently. It seems that this country will have many people have jobs to do, so it causes they often change old home electronic products or replaced them easily, when they have enough income to spend to buy any kinds of new home electronic products to use at homes easily. Moreover, their flowing old electronic home products behaviors also indicate that this country has many people their salaries may be increased in possible from their emplyers. When this country can have many different kinds of home electornic products are sold. It means that this country's electronic home products needs or demand had been increasing, due to many people have jobs to do and income increases to excite their living of needs also improve. Consequently, this country may seem have better economic improvement. We can observe from this country's electronic home products rubblish increasing income in theis period.

On conclusion, this country ought experience economic growth at this period. So, " flowing expensive electronic home rubblish increasing number " may seem that this country's economic growth is rapidly in this period, due to many people have jobs to do as well as salaries increase in this period.

www.ingramcontent.com/pod-product-compliance
Lightning Source LLC
Chambersburg PA
CBHW021544150726
47990CB00006B/2387